ONE
CHURCH

Thomas Campbell, 1763-1854. Steel engraving based on the portrait by Thomas Sully, widely distributed in books and prints, often carrying a facsimile autograph, Your Affectionate Father, Thomas Campbell.

ONE CHURCH

A Bicentennial Celebration of
Thomas Campbell's
Declaration & Address

GLENN THOMAS CARSON, DOUGLAS A. FOSTER
& CLINTON J. HOLLOWAY, EDITORS

LEAFWOOD
PUBLISHERS
Abilene, Texas

One Church
A Bicentennial Celebration of
Thomas Campbell's *Declaration and Address*

L E A F W O O D
P U B L I S H E R S

Copyright 2008 by Disciples of Christ Historical Society

ISBN 978-0-89112-565-5

Printed in the United States of America

Scripture quotations, unless otherwise noted, are from The Holy Bible,
New International Version. Copyright 1984, International Bible Society.
Used by permission of Zondervan Publishers.

Cover design by Rick Gibson

Illustrations provided by Mac Ice and Elaine Philpott, Disciples of Christ Historical Society,
and by Clinton J. Holloway, Nashville, Tennessee.

For information contact:
Leafwood Publishers, Abilene, Texas
1-877-816-4455 toll free
www.leafwoodpublishers.com

08 09 10 11 12 / 7 6 5 4 3 2 1

"We look forward into the new century that lies before us with...a prayer for God's continued guidance, and a prophecy that vastly greater things are to be accomplished under God in the century to come than have been achieved in the century past, and those who join in celebrating our second Centennial will have occasion for thanksgiving to Almighty God for the realization of aims and ends which neither our fathers before us, nor we of to-day, have been permitted to see, except by faith."

—J. H. GARRISON, Chairman, Centennial Campaign Committee, *Program of the International Centennial Celebration and Conventions of the Disciples of Christ*, Pittsburgh, Pennsylvania, 1909, page 16.

Contents

THOMAS CAMPBELL

1763-1854

THE CHURCH OF CHRIST
UPON EARTH IS ESSENTIALLY,
INTENTIONALLY, AND
CONSTITUTIONALLY ONE

WHERE THE SCRIPTURES
SPEAK, WE SPEAK;
WHERE THE SCRIPTURES
ARE SILENT, WE ARE SILENT

Cenotaph in the courtyard of Disciples of Christ Historical Society, Nashville, Tennessee, by Sculptor Puryear Mims, c. 1958. Executed in granite, the monument depicts the Campbells, Barton Stone, and Walter Scott in bas-relief, together with their notable quotes.

Introduction

Thomas Campbell stood at the rail of the ship and breathed deeply of the invigorating ocean breeze. He was leaving his beloved Ireland and setting sail for America. Perhaps there his health would improve. Perhaps there the religious air would be healthier too—free from the strife and division that had troubled him so in the Seceder Presbyterian Church.

Upon his arrival in America in 1807 the 44-year-old minister was appointed to preach in western Pennsylvania by the American counterpart of the Anti-Burgher Seceder Presbyterian Church. His hopes for a better religious climate were quickly dashed. He found in the new land the same bitter, narrow sectarianism. When he invited Presbyterians who were not part of his church to the communion table one Sunday, he was expelled from the denomination.

In a cordial meeting of fellow Christians held at Buffalo, Pennsylvania, August 17, 1809, the Christian Association of Washington, Pennsylvania, was formed "for the sole purpose of promoting simple, evangelical Christianity, free from all mixture of human opinions and inventions of men." They did not see themselves as a church but rather as "voluntary advocates for church reformation." The *Declaration and Address* of this Christian Association was written by Thomas Campbell and approved for publication on September 7, 1809.

The document consisted of a brief "declaration" listing nine objectives of the Christian Association and a lengthy "address" that included thirteen bold propositions for Christian unity. The "grand design" of Thomas

Campbell and the Christian Association was to "reconcile and unite men to God and to each other, in truth and love, to the glory of God." Religious division was seen as the great barrier to this grand design. Campbell described these "bitter jarrings and janglings" as "sad," "accursed," "woeful," and "hapless." Proposition 12 of the *Declaration and Address* calls division among Christians "a horrid evil, fraught with many evils." Division, declared Campbell, is anti-Christian, anti-scriptural, and anti-natural.

Christian unity is the clarion call of the *Declaration and Address*. It called for "a permanent Scriptural unity among the Churches, upon the solid basis of universally acknowledged and self-evident truths"—a "visible unity in truth and holiness, in faith and love." At the heart of the irenic document is Proposition 1: "THAT the Church of Christ upon earth is essentially, intentionally, and constitutionally one; consisting of all those in every place that profess their faith in Christ and obedience to Him in all things according to the Scriptures, and that manifest the same by their tempers and conduct, and none else; as none else can be truly and properly called Christians."

The Bible and the Bible alone would be the "Divine Standard." The objective would be "the restoration of a Christian and brotherly intercourse with one another"—"an entire union of all the Churches in faith and practice, according to the word of God." This effort at reform would be a Christ-centered, Bible-based movement. "Christ alone being the head, the center; his word the rule; an explicit belief of, and manifest conformity to it in all things, the terms." Furthermore, "nothing ought to be inculcated upon Christians as articles of faith; nor required of them as terms of communion, but what is expressly taught and enjoined upon them in the word of God."

Fervent prayer and earnest efforts were expected of all who sought to answer Jesus' prayer for unity in John 17. "Are we not all praying for that happy event, when there shall be but one fold, as there is but one Chief Shepherd? What! Shall we pray for a thing and not strive to obtain it! not use the necessary means to have it accomplished!" "Duty then is ours; but events belong to God." Perhaps the most poignant words of the *Declaration and Address* are Campbell's plea to ministers and members alike. "O! that ministers and people would but consider that there are no divisions in the grave, nor in that world which lies beyond it! there our divisions must come to an end! we must all unite there! Would to God that we could find it in our hearts to put an end to our short-lived divisions here; that so we might leave a blessing behind us; even a happy and united Church!"

Those words still ring in our ears, for 2009 marks the two hundredth anniversary of Thomas Campbell's *Declaration and Address*. This new call for Christian reformation and unity on the occasion of this special anniversary should be welcomed by all in what is sometimes called the Stone-Campbell Movement. It gives us an opportunity to revisit, reexamine, and restudy the deep longing that drove Thomas Campbell to write such a remarkable document. The simple principles leading to Christian unity espoused by Thomas Campbell in 1809 are still relevant, perhaps even more so, in 2009, to those who are "promoting a pure, evangelical reformation."

The reader will surely enjoy Clinton J. Holloway's anecdotal bicentennial essay "Essentially, Intentionally and Constitutionally One: A Brief History of Thomas Campbell's *Declaration and Address*." The reader will surely marvel at Douglas A. Foster's eminently readable "Modern Restating of the

13 Propositions of the *Declaration and Address* of Thomas Campbell." But there is more in store. Six thoughtful (and sometimes provocative) essays produced by writers from a wide spectrum of the Stone-Campbell Movement earnestly seek to apply the principles of the *Declaration and Address* to a modern audience. The essays show just how relevant and timely the *Declaration and Address* really is. As one writer put it, "We recognize that this document, written in a much earlier time, is anything but antiquated. Perhaps now more than ever the clarion call for unity among God's people connects with a culture frustrated with division, hatred and war."

And, in keeping with the proposed "Great Communion" on Sunday, October 4, 2009 (commemorating the 1909 "Great Communion" at the Centennial Convention held in Pittsburgh, Pennsylvania), there are brief but meaningful communion meditations written by men and women from Africa, Australia, India, Indonesia, and the United States. Remember that in the *Declaration and Address* Thomas Campbell called the Lord's Supper "that great ordinance of unity and love!" Throughout this anniversary publication the reader will also find choice quotations from the original *Declaration and Address*.

We are indebted to the Disciples of Christ Historical Society for funding this project, to Leafwood Publishers for publishing this important new call in the spirit of the *Declaration and Address*, to the 2009 Task Force for their excellent contributions to this volume and the larger bicentennial events, and to the general editors for their diligent oversight: Glenn Thomas Carson, Douglas A. Foster, and Clinton J. Holloway.

VICTOR KNOWLES

PART I

Historical Events

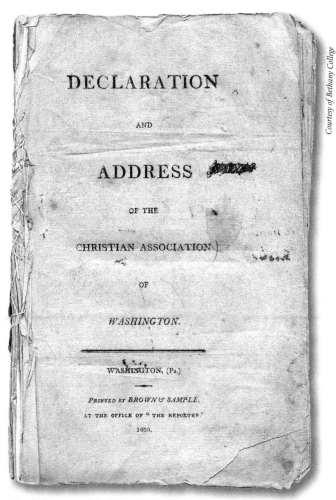

Proof sheet copy of *Declaration and Address of the Christian Association of Washington*. Printed in the office of the local paper, late September–early October 1809, the original copy, housed at Bethany College, shows emendations by both Thomas and Alexander Campbell.

Essentially, Intentionally, and Constitutionally One

A Brief History of Thomas Campbell's *Declaration and Address*

Clinton J. Holloway

Thomas Campbell's 1809 *Declaration and Address of the Christian Association of Washington*, popularly known as the *Declaration and Address*, has been called many things: a hundred years ahead of its time, a clarion call to reformation, our foundational document, the *Magna Charta* of the Movement, the source of our DNA. But it has also been called implausible and impractical, a pipe dream, wearisome reading, and a failure. In turns it has been virtually forgotten or largely ignored; and its centennial and bicentennial have been the cause for commemoration on a popular level. As the two hundredth anniversary of the document's debut is observed in 2009 it is incumbent upon the heirs of the Stone-Campbell Movement—those who trace a measure of their spiritual heritage to the document—to once again weigh its merit and value for the present generation. The essays in this book show that writers from across the American segments of the Movement have been asked to do just that, to observe from their own lives and ministries the relevance of a document written at the dawn of the nineteenth century.

This essay will take a brief and sometimes anecdotal journey back over those two hundred years to observe some of the highs and lows, the ebbs and flows, to see how the *Declaration and Address* has been received by those who have come before the present generations, as well as provide a brief historical survey of the document itself.

Part I
The Origin and Impact of the *Declaration and Address*

Thomas Campbell's life and the events of his ministry are recount-ed in a number of sources.[1] Neither space nor the focus of this volume allows for an in-depth biography of the man and his personal spiritual journey to become known as one of the four founding leaders of the reform movement that bears his name. There may be some merit, how-ever, in looking at events immediately preceding the writing of the *Dec-laration and Address* to understand what led the already reform-minded Irish minister to issue his call for reformation of the church.

Early in March 1807 Thomas Campbell left his home, family, and church in Ireland for the United States, arriving in Philadelphia after a thirty-five-day voyage on May 13, 1807.[2] Perhaps not coincidentally, Campbell found that the Associate Synod of North America was in session in that city—the leadership body of the Anti-Burgher Seceder Presbyterians, Campbell's sect. He presented his credentials and letters of introduction to the Synod and was cordially received and welcomed into fellowship. Campbell, at his own request, was appointed to serve the Presbytery of Chartiers in south-western Pennsylvania, where many friends and acquaintances from home had immigrated. By the end of June Thomas had arrived in Washington, Pennsylvania, and had received preaching assignments from the Chartiers Presbytery that extended through the end of October 1808. One of those assignments was to visit the distant village of Cannamaugh, above Pittsburgh, on the third and fourth Sabbaths of August. It was here that Thomas Campbell felt the full force of the divisions within the Presbyterian family. Here he allowed all members of the scattered fellowship, not just the Anti-Burgher stripe, to participate in the sacramental celebration, regardless of presbyterial connection.

> "THE CHURCH OF CHRIST UPON EARTH IS ESSENTIALLY, INTENTIONALLY, AND CONSTITUTIONALLY ONE"

News of Campbell's supposed heresy quickly circulated among the Anti-Burghers, leading to his suspension by the Chartiers Presbytery and eventual censure by the Associate Synod the following May. Afterward the censure was commuted to a "rebuke and admonition." On return to Washington in the early fall of 1808 Thomas Campbell found that, within the Presbytery, his ability and opportunity to minister had thus been compromised by the controversy and on September 13, 1808, submitted a paper to the Chartiers authorities in which he refused to accept their authority and withdrew from the Presbytery and the Associate Synod. As the Associate Synod met only once a year it was not until May of 1809 that the Synod, again meeting in Philadelphia, had a chance to act on Thomas Campbell's withdrawal. It was at this meeting of the Synod, on May 19, 1809, that

Thomas Campbell presented a paper entitled *Declaration and Address to the Associate Synod* which must certainly have contained at least a portion of the seminal principles of his later document of similar title. The paper was read but a deputation suggested that it be withdrawn because it offered proposals inconsistent with Seceder doctrine. As a result of these extended actions, Thomas Campbell formally and permanently severed his connections with the Seceder fellowship in the United States.

Though his ties to a formal denominational body were cut, Thomas Campbell had not withdrawn from his calling as a minister of the gospel. Throughout the controversy Campbell continued to preach and administer the Lord's Supper where he could, growing in popularity and the esteem of the community. By summer 1809 a meeting of like-minded persons had discussed the idea of forming a Christian Association, and at a second meeting at Buffalo, Washington County, on August 17, 1809, those who held the principles of Christian union, regardless of denominational affiliation constituted themselves as the Christian Association of Washington. A committee of twenty-one (probably all of those in attendance) agreed on the need for a statement of purpose and objectives. As spokesman for the group, Thomas Campbell was called upon to author the purpose statement, no doubt drawing upon his paper recently read at the Associate Synod meeting in Philadelphia.

In order to have time to prepare the document, Thomas Campbell retreated to the nearby home of a Dr. Welch to study and write. A brief *Declaration* was drawn up outlining nine points or purposes of the Association. That *Declaration* was followed by an *Address* and later an Appendix of about 23,000 words that more fully expressed the principles and objectives of the Christian Association.[3] The gist of the document is found in thirteen propositions that, taken as a whole, deplore the divisions of Christianity and set forth how the sin of division was to be eradicated. Proposition 1 coined the immortal phrase "that the church of Christ upon earth is essentially, intentionally, and constitutionally one...." At a meeting of the Washington Association on September 7, 1809, the *Declaration and Address of the Christian Association of Washington* was read and unanimously approved. Plans were made for publication at the expense of the society. Soon the printers, Brown and Sample of Washington, made a proof copy ready for Thomas to edit. In the meantime Thomas received word that his family, delayed in Scotland for a year because of a shipwreck, had arrived at the port of New York and were by now on their way to Washington via Philadelphia. After a separation of more than two years, Thomas Campbell made haste to meet his family on the way. Son Alexander, a young man now of twenty-one, was promptly shown the document and, as the story goes, promised his father to devote the rest of his life and energies to promoting the principles and views of the *Declaration and Address*.[4] Alexander therefore spent his first six months in the United States in intensive ministerial study under the tutelage of the Elder Campbell; the junior Campbell preached his first sermon before the Christian Association on July 15, 1810.[5]

In the meantime, publication of the *Declaration and Address* had been delayed until late December 1809 due to a lack of quality paper in the frontier town. It is unknown how many copies of the document Brown and Sample produced or how widely copies were distributed.[6] H. Eugene Johnson notes that the *Declaration and Address* was originally signed by both Thomas Campbell and Thomas Acheson, Secretary and Treasurer of the Christian Association respectively. Major General Acheson, a merchant by trade and the owner of a mansion on Washington's Main Street built that year, was one of the wealthiest and most influential men of western Pennsylvania. It is Johnson's assertion that Thomas Acheson's signature may have been added to lend prestige to the document.[7]

One biographer of Thomas Campbell says that the document was "scarcely noticed by the religious leaders of western Pennsylvania."[8] There are few, if any, known contemporary accounts of how the *Declaration and Address* was received by the religious community. One clue to its reception comes from Thomas Campbell himself, writing in the *Millennial Harbinger* in 1839 as a response to a Christian Union meeting held in New York. Campbell wrote, "Some thirty years ago, when we addressed a portion of our fellow Christians, in Western Pennsylvania, upon this all-important subject, we met with universal opposition from the leaders of the people, and were considered as disturbers of religious society...." Later in the same article the Elder Campbell states further that in the intervening three decades "we have been most bitterly opposed by the leaders of all parties, Atheistic, Deistic, Catholic and Protestant, with which we have happened to come into contact."[9]

Robert Richardson, in his monumental *Memoirs of Alexander Campbell*, devoted a large portion of one chapter to the *Declaration and Address*, and comments on its reception in the religious community:

The ministers of the different parties around, to whom copies were sent, received them apparently with silent acquiescence as to the principles laid down, not a single one of them venturing a public reply, though earnestly and repeatedly invited to consider carefully the propositions submitted, and to make any corrections or amendments which might occur to them, and assured that all objections presented in writing would be "thankfully received and seriously considered with all due attention."

Courtesy of Bethany College

Impressing Artifact – Printing press of Brown and Sample, Washington, Pennsylvania, upon which the *Declaration and Address* was printed in 1809. For many years the press stood in the lobby of the local paper, the *Observer-Reporter*. It is now in a nearby museum.

Richardson's explanation for why there was no public comment or rebuttal to the "pamphlet" was that either the local clergy could find no "vulnerable point of attack" or that the humble Christian spirit and affectionate manner in which the subject was discussed "disarmed resentment."[10]

As another indicator of how poorly the *Declaration and Address* was received in the religious community, we do know that in October 1810 when the Presbyterian Synod of Pittsburgh met in Washington, Pennsylvania, they refused the request of Thomas Campbell and the Christian Association for admittance to the Presbyterian Church in the United States of America saying that such efforts at reform, though appearing sound, rather promoted division instead of union.[11] It was perhaps this decision that helped to set the future course of the infant reform movement. Having been denied fellowship in the Presbyterian Church, the Christian Association and its leadership realized they must become more than a loose association of believers and thus formed themselves into an independent congregation constituted on May 4, 1811. In less than six weeks, in the valley of Brush Run, a rough log building was erected thereby giving the name to the first congregation of the Movement: the Brush Run Church. The experimental Christian Association of Washington had lasted less than two years.

"IT IS HIGH TIME FOR US NOT ONLY TO THINK, BUT ALSO TO ACT"

With the demise of the Christian Association of Washington, the *Declaration and Address,* the document outlining the principles and justification for the organization, seems also to have languished. The postscript to the document, added after the final approval by the association, called for the establishment of a monthly paper to be known as the *Christian Monitor*, to promote the reform principles of the Christian Association. It was to commence in early 1810 as soon as five hundred annual subscriptions could be obtained. As we know that no paper appeared among the eastern reformers until Alexander Campbell first issued the *Christian Baptist* in 1823, we can assume that the five hundred subscribers never materialized or rather that once the association became a church the plan may have been abandoned altogether.

That the *Declaration and Address* and its principles of Christian unity had fallen on deaf ears in the religious community, outside his own small band of followers, must have been a tremendous disappointment for Thomas Campbell. However, it cannot be counted out as a total failure. The *Declaration and Address* succeeded in attracting the interest and energy of one man: Alexander Campbell. It would be in the son that Thomas Campbell's *Declaration and Address* would have the most profound impact, soon eclipsing even the father's own influence and considerable efforts at reform. True to his word, the *Declaration and Address* would be the genesis for Alexander's life work, to which he devoted his time, near limitless energy, and vast mental resources: the promotion of his earthly father's vision for Christian unity reflecting the Heavenly Father's imperative for unity (John 17:21). At the time of his death in 1866, after nearly six decades of labor, the Movement and principles to which Alexander Campbell had devoted his life could boast a quarter of a million adherents across the United States and influence that reached at least half a dozen countries.[12]

It is probably accurate to say that the *Declaration and Address* itself had little direct influence upon the first and second generations of the Movement because they simply did not have access to it. Rather, the impact of the document came largely through the author himself—his own preaching and teaching in subsequent years. Certainly the greater impact of the *Declaration and Address* came about as it was funneled through the interpretive skills of Alexander Campbell's speaking and writing as a means to promote the reform principles. There is no question but that Thomas Campbell's contributions to the founding of the Movement were quickly and swiftly eclipsed by the star shine of his son. However, if no one else recognized Thomas Campbell's Moses-like role in the founding of the Movement, at least his Joshua understood. In the preface to his 1835 *Christian System*, Alexander Campbell cites the *Declaration and Address* as the "constitutional principle" of the Christian Association, and that the *Christian System*, after a quarter of a century of toil and strife, was an effort to place the *capital principles* of the Movement before the community in a "plain, definite and perspicuous style."[13] Of his father's influence upon his life, Alexander Campbell wrote in the preface to Thomas Campbell's memoirs, "...whatever good, little or much, I may have achieved under God, I owe it all, and those benefited by it, owe it all, to his paternal care and instruction, and especially to his example."[14]

Lester G. McAllister, in his biographical essay on Thomas Campbell for the 2004 *Encyclopedia of the Stone-Campbell Movement*, says:

In most writings concerning the Stone-Campbell Movement, Thomas [Campbell] all but disappears historically after the publication in 1809 of his important statement on Christian unity, the Declaration and Address. Through the succeeding years, however, he remained a wise counselor and guide for his son and others in the Movement. The father and son complemented each other in personality and intellect.[15]

Part II
Two Hundred Years of the *Declaration and Address*

After the limited press run of 1809, the *Declaration and Address* was not seen again in print for fifty years. In 1861 Alexander Campbell reproduced it in his *Memoirs of Elder Thomas Campbell*. Even the more succinct "13 Propositions" were not widely reissued in either the *Christian Baptist* or *Millennial Harbinger*, save for one 1839 article in the *Harbinger* in which Thomas Campbell reprints eight of the propositions in an article commending a "Christian Union Convention" held in New York, saying "we greatly rejoice that this all-important subject of Christian union is beginning to awake the public attention...throughout Christendom."[16]

Save for its appearance in the *Memoirs* in 1861 and again in 1871, it would not be until the early twentieth century, when the document was one hundred years old, that the *Declaration and Address* would enjoy a wide circulation, when perhaps as many as thirty thousand copies were reproduced in connection with the 1909 International Centennial Celebration and Conventions that were held in Pittsburgh, Pennsylvania, to mark the occasion. As the *Declaration and Address* became more readily available, the twentieth century saw significant interest in the document with several interpretive volumes, essays, and synopses appearing in the years of its second century. With the advent of the computer age late in the century, the *Declaration and Address* is now accessible to anyone in the world with Internet access.

The following is a brief outline of some of the major highlights and anecdotes in the history of the *Declaration and Address*. It is in no way intended to be comprehensive but gives a broad overview of interpretations and appearances.

1809 Thomas Campbell wrote the *Declaration and Address*. The printer presented the proofs to Thomas Campbell by October. This proof copy was also reviewed by Alexander Campbell when he and the family arrived in Washington and shows evidence of editing by both Thomas and Alexander Campbell. The original passed from Thomas, to Alexander, to his daughter, Decima Campbell Barclay, who allowed it to be reproduced by zinc etching in anticipation of the 1909 Centennial Convention, where the original was the "chief exhibit." After 1909 Decima passed it on to her son, Julian Barclay. Julian sold the original document to Edward N. Clopper, who then presented it to Bethany College. It is housed in Archives and Special Collections of the T. W. Phillips Memorial Library, Bethany

College, Bethany, West Virginia. This copy is pictured in the *Encyclopedia of the Stone-Campbell Movement.*

1809 Very late in the year Brown and Sample printed the *Declaration and Address* in Washington, Pennsylvania, at the offices of "The Reporter." Lack of quality paper delayed publication for some time. Given that fact, and the relatively small population of the area, it is easy to speculate that perhaps only a few dozen copies were printed. Only one original unbound copy is presently known to exist and comes from the library of Thomas Benjamin Knowles. It is housed in Archives and Special Collections of the T.W. Phillips Memorial Library, Bethany

"TAKING THE DIVINE WORD ALONE FOR OUR RULE"

College, Bethany, West Virginia. [17] This copy is pictured in *Alexander Campbell: Adventurer in Freedom*, Volume 1, by Eva Jean Wrather.

1861 Alexander Campbell issued *Memoirs of Elder Thomas Campbell* compiled with the assistance of his sister, Dorothea Bryant. The *Memoirs* are thought to be the first time the *Declaration and Address* had been reprinted in fifty years, for the first time giving members of the Stone-Campbell Movement broad access to the document. The *Memoirs* contain about a page of "footnotes" by Alexander Campbell explaining certain passages as well as an essay by Dr. Archibald Campbell covering a few details of the life of Thomas Campbell in the twenty--year period following the appearance of the *Declaration and Address* and citing the slow growth of the reform movement in this period. The *Memoirs* were reprinted in 1871. This version, sometimes called the "second edition," contains edits to the original said to come from the pen of Thomas Campbell as well as emendations made by Alexander Campbell. Comparison of the two editions by Ernie Stefanik showed 2,760 corrections from the first to the second version, of which slightly more than one hundred can be attributed to Thomas Campbell.[18]

1868 Robert Richardson's *Memoirs of Alexander Campbell* devoted a chapter to the *Declaration and Address* which included the thirteen propositions. As the official biographer of Alexander Campbell and long-time colleague and physician to the Campbell family, Robert Richardson had access to the Campbell family papers enjoyed by no one else in history. His two-volume biography of Alexander Campbell remains the definitive resource.[19]

1904 *Historical Documents Advocating Christian Union* was compiled by Charles Alexander Young, then the Managing Editor of *The Christian Century*; it contained the *Declaration and Address,* which he called the greatest document ever written in the advocacy of Christian Union. *The Declaration and Address* is prefaced by a substantial analysis by Errett Gates, which first appeared as a series of articles in the *Christian Century.* Gates said that there was never a time when the principles laid out in the *Declaration and Address* were more in need of enunciation than at the beginning of the twentieth century. [20]

1909 In the years leading up to 1909 a Centennial Committee was formed to plan a great convention to celebrate the one hundredth anniversary of the *Declaration and Address,* then understood as the genesis of the Movement. W. R. Warren gave leadership to the event and brought it to amazing fruition; some 25,000 people gathered for the Centennial Convention in Pittsburgh, Pennsylvania, October 11-19, 1909.[21] The climax of the event was a communion service at Forbes Field, perhaps the largest in history to that date. The "chief exhibit" at the Convention was Thomas Campbell's proof sheet copy of the *Declaration and Address* on loan from Decima Campbell Barclay. A limited number of zinc etching reprints of the proof sheet copy showing quill pen editing by Thomas Campbell and other emendations by Alexander Campbell were produced, bound in leather, and distributed.[22] The special edition was published by the Record Publishing Company, Coraopolis, Pennsylvania.

The Centennial Bureau also produced a paperback "Centennial Edition" of the *Declaration and Address* for popular consumption that reproduced the original line by line, word for word without the edit marks, even duplicating the typeface. Also produced by the Record Publishing Company, some copies say "twentieth thousand" and others say "thirtieth thousand," indicating the wide dissemination of the document during its centenary.

Standard Publishing also issued a reprint of the *Declaration and Address* in 1909 to help celebrate "Declaration Day" in conjunction with the Convention. The small paperback volume, titled *A Plea for Christian Union,* also contained other information relative to Christian union. Herbert Moninger, Standard's Bible School Editor, promoted the book as a teaching tool for the local church. "Many will hear the plea for the restoration of the New Testament for the first time, and will want to carry home something that will tell them more about it," he opined. When ordered in quantities the book sold for ten cents.[23] With these two editions available in 1909, for the first time in the history of the Movement, the *Declaration and Address* made it into the hands of the average person in the pew who was able to read, perhaps for the first time, the historic plea for Christian unity.

Dean E. Walker, in his *Adventuring for Christian Unity,* said in 1935 that the *Declaration and Address* was over a century before its time, a sentiment that was often repeated in the early twentieth century.[24] If that is true, then perhaps the 1909 Centennial marked a renaissance for the document, the beginning of a new era in which the principles of restoration and Christian unity would find a wider audience and a greater impact than had been known in the previous century.

Following the 1909 Centennial Celebration, Standard Publishing published a 600-page *Centennial Convention Report* reproducing the speeches and

An estimated 25,000 people gathered in Pittsburgh's Forbes Field at 3 o'clock on the afternoon of October 17, 1909, for the Communion Service of the Centennial Celebration, thought to be the largest communion service in American history to date. 500 deacons and 100 elders served from 50 tables. Afterwards the tables, cups, and plates were sold as souvenirs.

sermons given over the course of the week-and-a-half assembly, including five speeches titled "Thomas Campbell and the Principles He Promulgated." One of those speeches was by Christian Women's Board of Missions Corresponding Secretary Effie Cunningham of Indianapolis, Indiana. Another was by Herbert Lockwood Willett of Chicago, a prominent liberal in the "higher criticism" controversies. Unsuccessfully, many had attempted to block Willett's appearance on the Centennial platform. In the Publisher's Note to the *Centennial Report*, Russell Errett, owner of Standard Publishing, went on record as disclaiming responsibility for Willett's name appearing in the volume.[25]

50,000 bronze badges were cast for those attending the October 11-19, 1909, International Centennial Celebration and Convention of the Disciples of Christ. The pin bar showed the Brush Run Church. Suspended from it with gold and black silk ribbon was the Convention emblem depicting the "four great Pioneers." Thomas Campbell is upper left. The reverse reads THAT THEY MAY ALL BE ONE, THAT THE WORLD MAY BELIEVE.

1923 The first book-length interpretation and analysis of the *Declaration and Address* appeared in 1923 under the title *The Christian Union Overture: An Interpretation of the Declaration and Address of Thomas Campbell* by Frederick Doyle Kershner, former President of Milligan College (Tennessee). Kershner said in his preface that though the *Declaration and Address* had been republished a number of times it had "never been revised or put into such a form as to make it easy reading for a twentieth century student." As "Christian Union" was then enjoying, according to Kershner, a renewed emphasis, it seemed worthwhile to present the *Declaration and Address* in a form intended to be more appealing than older editions. "Such commentary as this book contains," said Kershner, "has been designed to make its original meaning clear and also to interpret that meaning in light of the development of the last hundred years."[26] In another context Kershner said of the *Declaration and Address*, "there is pure gold in it, but it requires earnest delving in order to bring it forth to the light of the day."[27] Kershner's interpretation was so popular that it remained the standard for the next several generations, particularly as Kershner served for more than twenty years as Dean of Butler School of Religion (now Christian Theological Seminary) in Indianapolis.

1935 P.H. Welshimer, minister of Canton, Ohio's First Christian Church, then the largest congregation in the Movement, released an easy-to-read volume of about two hundred pages titled *Concerning the Disciples, A Brief Resume of the Movement to Restore the New Testament Church.* One of the most respected ministers in the Movement and a leader in the emerging conservative Movement among Disciples, Welshimer's book was a nationwide call to teach Restoration History to youth and an effort for renewed study of the principles and events of the Movement. In his two-and-a-half page chapter on the *Declaration and Address,* Welshimer succinctly quotes only the thirteen propositions as the crux of the thirty-thousand-word document.[28]

1949 To mark the one hundredth anniversary of the founding of the American Christian Missionary Society, its descendant, the International

Convention of the Disciples of Christ, issued a paperback edition of the *Declaration and Address*, together with *The Last Will and Testament of the Springfield Presbytery*, with a brief introduction to both documents by Frederick D. Kershner. This edition was later reprinted at least three times by Bethany Press ((1955, 1960, 1967) and at least once, if not more, by Karl Ketcherside's *Mission Messenger* in 1972. These editions put the *Declaration and Address* into the hands of countless students and church members through much of the mid-twentieth century.

1951 William Robinson, leader in theological training for generations of British Churches of Christ, educator at Overdale College, Birmingham, England, and later at Christian Theological Seminary, Indianapolis, Indiana, issued an edition of the *Declaration and Address* for the British churches in 1951 which was reprinted at least twice. Robinson, too, called the document "a century before its time." In his introduction Robinson noted that Thomas Campbell had high hopes that his document would produce a religious revolution within a few years. Since Campbell was before his time, however, he was disappointed that his work was, in effect, to set up one more church among many. Robinson believed that both the British and American churches were born out of a passion for Christian unity, and that the closeness between the countries was nurtured in the nineteenth century by the

> "WHAT SHOULD DETER US FROM …AN ENTIRE UNION OF ALL THE CHURCHES?"

writings of Alexander Campbell and his 1847 visit to Great Britain, and in the twentieth century by the work of the World Convention of Churches of Christ. Robinson felt that the Address, the main body of the *Declaration and Address* (pages 24–54 in the original edition) was "in these days of more terse expression...wearisome reading." As a result, in his own edition he offered a three-page digest of the Appendix, thereby shortening the document considerably.[29]

1971–1972 Tampa, Florida, attorney and theologian, H. Eugene Johnson released a small book in 1971 titled *The Declaration and Address for Today.* Citing that it had been nearly fifty years since Kershner's analysis and that "the world had turned over a few times since 1923," Johnson felt that the "immortal document" deserved an interpretation for "our times." He observed that most of Thomas Campbell's literary jewels were not "clearly labeled and neatly stacked" so that "consequently much lip service is given to the *Declaration and Address* but few dig into its depth."[30] After a brief summary of the document (he does not reprint the original document), Johnson devoted chapters to the themes of organic unity, the foundation of unity, creedal abuse of unity, Campbell's use of scripture, and the Latitudinarian Spirit of Love.

"WHY SHOULD WE DEEM IT A THING INCREDIBLE THAT THE CHURCH SHOULD RESUME THAT ORIGINAL UNITY?"

The following year at Emmanuel School of Religion, Johnson City, Tennessee, Johnson was invited to deliver two lectures in which he explored whether the basic principles set out by Thomas Campbell in the *Declaration and Address* were still relevant. His conclusion was that a vigorous application of the principles to our "present situation" may lead us again into an "adventure for Christian Unity."[31] The two lectures, "Relation of Christ, scripture and Unity" and "Role of Love, Life and Unity," were later bound together and made available by the author under the title *The Current Reformation: Thoughts from Thomas Campbell.*

1976 During the last decades of the twentieth century, when it was felt that there were fewer and fewer who seemed committed to the ideals of the Stone-Campbell Restoration Movement, College Press of Joplin, Missouri, began a systematic effort to make available early works of the through their Restoration Reprint series and to make those key resources more accessible through the publication of indices and paraphrases.[32] Knofel Staton, then a professor at Ozark Christian College in Joplin, undertook to complete a paraphrase of the *Declaration and Address*, reducing it by about half and putting it in a modern English form, which College Press then published. Many late twentieth-century schools and students have benefited from Dr. Staton's paraphrase, using either it or various photocopies of the *Declaration and Address* in their classroom studies.[33]

1997 Ernest C. "Ernie" Stefanik of Derry, Pennsylvania, and Dr. Hans Rollmann of Memorial University of Newfoundland, St. John's, Canada, made the *Declaration and Address*, in its first and second edition and paraphrase, available in electronic format on the Internet thereby granting worldwide access to the documents for the first time.

Stefanik has done the Movement and advocates of Christian union a great service by preparing the various documents for Internet publication and by analyzing the various textual variants from the original Thomas Campbell edition to the subsequent reprintings by Alexander Campbell and others.[34]

That same year, an Internet seminar was convened on the Stone-Campbell History List hosted by the Bible Department of Abilene (Texas) Christian University as an experiment in sustained, formal investigation and conversation on topics of historical and theological interest. Various individuals submitted papers on the *Declaration and Address,* generating considerable discussion, suggestions, and criticism. These essays from the online seminar were eventually reprinted in book form (see below). The electronic versions of the *Declaration and Address* were updated in 2003.

2000 Growing out of the online seminar noted above, Thomas H. Olbricht and Hans Rollmann edited a substantial, scholarly, limited-circulation volume of essays, bibliography of Thomas Campbell, and a reprint of the first edition of the *Declaration and Address* under the title *The Quest for Christian Unity, Peace, and Purity in Thomas Campbell's Declaration and Address: Text and Studies.*[35] Among the twenty or so essays several topics are discussed, including one by Paul M. Blowers on the interpretations of the document by Frederick Kershner and William Robinson, noted previously. Ernie Stefanik provided the text of the *Declaration and Address* itself, as well as essays on textual variations, external history of the document, and a bibliography citing the major editions and reprintings.

2003 *The Encyclopedia of the Stone-Campbell Movement* contains an entry on the *Declaration and Address* and a brief bibliography by Paul M. Blowers and William J. Richardson, and pictures Thomas Campbell's own copy of the document. A four-page biographical entry on Thomas Campbell was contributed by Lester G. McAllister. The *Declaration and Address* can be said to be the impetus and genesis for most everything else found in the volume as the foundational document of the Christian reformation movement now known as the Stone-Campbell Movement.[36]

2005 A Task Force composed of Doug Foster, Linda Chenoweth, Robert Welsh, Glenn Thomas Carson, Mark Taylor, Clinton J. Holloway, and Jeff Weston was called together in September by the Stone-Campbell Dialogue and Disciples of Christ Historical Society to begin formulating appropriate ways of commemorating the 2009 Bicentennial of Thomas Campbell's *Declaration and Address.* The following year the Task Force was expanded to include sixteen members, five from each of the three major U.S. streams of the Movement, with Australian Jeff Weston, Executive Director of World Convention, lending an international voice. The major emphasis in marking the bicentenary is the unity we share in the Stone-Campbell Movement at the Lord's Supper.

> "WITH YOU ALL WE DESIRE TO UNITE IN THE BONDS OF AN ENTIRE CHRISTIAN UNITY"

Under the Task Force leadership the commemoration will commence at the 17th World Convention in 2008 in Nashville, Tennessee, and will culminate the first Sunday in October 2009. A global observance is encouraged through various materials available online at www.greatcommunion.com.

The Declaration and Address was a nineteenth-century call for the unity of believers based on the commitment to Jesus Christ shared by all Christians. The specifics of the document reflect the time in which it was written in its assumptions and style. Many certainly would judge its proposals to be naïve. Yet the breathtaking vision of Christians loving, worshiping, and serving together in every locality—allowing the Spirit of Christ to form them into humble servants—is one for which increasing numbers of believers long. This vision is today the major thrust of movements all across Christianity. A reappropriation of the spirit of *The Declaration and Address* in the churches of the Stone-Campbell Movement may be one of the richest contributions we can make to the emerging world of Christianity.

A Contemporary Restating of the 13 Propositions

Douglas A. Foster

The following propositions are by no means intended to be a creed or something to be imposed on believers—nothing could be further from the truth. They are designed, rather, to focus our hearts and minds on the great question of what it means to be followers of Christ. Too often we seem to have forgotten what is central to our identity as Christians and as Christ's church. It is our hope that these ideas will stimulate serious consideration of who we are and who we ought to be.

Proposition 1

Christ established one church—just one. This church is made up of everyone who has faith in Christ and is trying to follow him in the ways God's Spirit in scripture has told us, and who others can see are being transformed into his likeness by the way they act. No one else has a right to be called a Christian.

Proposition 2

It is physically impossible for all Christians to be together in one place to worship and work, so there have to be local groups of Christians that reflect the culture, language, and context of each place. These groups will not all look, think, or act alike, yet they are all part of Christ's church and ought to recognize it. They must accept and embrace each other just as Christ has accepted each of us. This will happen when Christians have the mind of Christ—that is, when they are willing to give themselves for those Christ died to redeem. This is the rule of Christ. This and this alone will join them perfectly.

Proposition 3

Therefore, nothing should be required to recognize, fellowship, embrace, work, worship, and be fully and visibly united with all Christians that is not specifically made a requirement by God in his word. Nothing should be required in the way local bodies of Christians operate that is not specifically required by Christ and his Apostles for the church. Furthermore, the chief requirements for full fellowship that God has decreed are our love for God and for people. This love is formed by our understanding of God's love for us shown through Christ.

Proposition 4

Both the Old and New Testaments are essential parts of the revelation of God's nature and work. They cannot be separated. While it is true that the practices required in the Old Testament (sacrifices, temple worship, priesthood, etc.) are not in force for Christians and that the good news of God's saving work is found fully in the New Testament, both testaments teach us about God's nature and work. The Bible is not primarily a constitution that functions as a legal document to consult in legal disputes. It is, instead, the sword of the Spirit; it is a place where we encounter God's

Spirit and are transformed increasingly into the likeness of Christ. Attending to scripture is essential to the visible unity of Christ's church.

Proposition 5

The Bible does not spell out in detail everything Christians are supposed to think, do or be—that is just not the nature of scripture. When there are specific actions Christians are told to take, there is almost never a set of detailed requirements for how to do it. Humans often want more detail and try to expand on the specifics, often making them requirements for accepting other Christians or groups of Christians. That is wrong. Again, Christians are those who say they are Christians and who show that they are by the way they live. No one should be allowed to require anything for recognition and fellowship that is outside of scripture and its work of transformation.

> "THE PROPOSITIONS ARE...DESIGNED FOR OPENING UP THE WAY"

Proposition 6

God gave us our ability to think and reason—that is a good thing. If, however, in the process of using our reason we come to conclusions that other Christians do not reach, and that causes us to reject them, we have been deceived by the evil one. Our pride has taken over and stopped our continued growth into the mind of Christ—a mind of complete humility and self-sacrifice. Human reason is not the ultimate standard for truth. Christians ought to be growing constantly in their understanding of the profound truths of the gospel—that's part of our spiritual growth as communities. But requiring or even expecting others to be where you are is not conducive to the visible unity Christ so much wants.

Proposition 7

Again, it is a good thing to use the intellectual abilities God has given us to plumb the depths of the marvelous truths of God. It is a good thing to think, and struggle and write about these matters. Individual Christians and Christian communities can and should draw great benefit in their spiritual growth from such efforts. Statements of belief can be very helpful in drawing our minds to the unspeakable riches and blessings we have been given and of which we can and should tell others. However, we must realize that such statements are the product of our human reasoning which, like everything else human, is not perfect. Even when we reach a mature level of doctrinal understanding, we need to remind ourselves constantly that there will always be Christians at all maturity levels—but they are still all Christians!

"TAKE UP THINGS JUST AS THE APOSTLES LEFT THEM"

Proposition 8

Once again, having an understanding of every Christian truth is not a requirement to be a Christian, a part of Christ's church. No one who is trying to follow Christ ought to be forced to confess any belief beyond what they understand and know. All a person needs to know to be part of Christ's church is that they are lost and that salvation is through Christ. When they confess that they believe in Christ and that they want to obey him fully according to his word—nothing else can be required.

Proposition 9

Everyone who confesses belief in Christ and commits to obey him, and who shows the reality of their commitment by the way they live, should consider each other as the precious saints of God, should love each other as sisters and brothers, children of the same family and Father, temples of the same Spirit, members of the same body, subjects of the same grace, objects of the same divine love bought with the same price, and joint heirs of the same inheritance. Whoever God has joined together this way, no one should dare divide.

Proposition 10

Division among Christians is a sickening evil, filled with many evils. It is anti-Christian because it destroys the visible unity of the body of Christ. It is as if Christ were cutting off parts of himself and throwing them away from the rest of his body! What a ludicrous picture! Division is anti-scriptural, since Christ himself specifically prohibited it, making it a direct violation of Christ's will. It is anti-natural, because it makes Christians condemn, hate and oppose one another—people who are actually obligated in the strongest way to love each other as sisters and brothers, just like Christ loved them. In other words, division repudiates everything Christianity is supposed to stand for.

Proposition 11

Two things are responsible for all the divisions and corruptions in Christ's church through the centuries. One is a neglect or even fundamental misunderstanding of God's will for us in scripture—that we have the mind of Christ and be transformed into his likeness. The other comes from the first. Some Christians, assuming they are "right," that they have gotten the "facts" perfectly, have assumed the authority to impose their conclusions on others as terms of recognition and fellowship.

Proposition 12

In reality, everything needed for the church to reach the highest state of perfection and purity on earth is first to receive as members only those who have understood their lostness and confessed their faith in Christ and commitment to follow him according to scripture; second, to keep as members only those who show those commitments in their everyday lives; and third, to see that ministers who reflect these ideals, preach only what is clearly taught in scripture. Finally, they must stick close to what scripture makes primary, seen in the example of the early church in the New Testament, without being distracted or corrupted by human tendencies toward pride and control.

Proposition 13

Finally, in every body of Christians decisions must be made about precisely how to conduct its work and worship. Scripture does not dictate such details. Whatever the best way of doing things for the local context should be adopted. These procedures, however, should always be understood as expedients or conveniences for that time and place. Others who do things differently should never be denigrated or condemned for such things, and when decisions are made to do things differently in the future, such changes should never be an issue of fighting or division.

The nature of these propositions is a call—a call to all followers of Christ today to be what Christ wants us to be. Christ's church does not reflect the reality of the one body. We have not maintained the unity of the Spirit in the bond of peace. It is easy to be complacent about our divisions because they seem to work. Yet the fractured nature of the body is a scandal—it hinders the world from believing, it dissipates the efforts of Christians to serve, and distracts believers from their own spiritual development. We are impelled to say these things. We have heard again the admonition from Isaiah 57:14—"Remove every obstruction from my people's way." It is the sincere intention of these propositions and of the essays that follow to bring to the attention of Christians fundamental truths and first principles that will lead us toward a permanent unity. How far that goal is reached now remains with the readers.

> "THE NEW TESTAMENT IS A PERFECT CONSTITUTION FOR WORSHIP"

Original Daguerreotype photograph taken about 1853 of Thomas Campbell at ninety years of age. Thought to be the only photograph of Father Campbell, it shows him with long, white hair. The original is now in the possession of the Disciples of Christ Historical Society.

PART 2
Contemporary Reflections

The *Declaration and Address* for a New Millennium

Rick Grover

As we observe the two-hundredth anniversary of Thomas Campbell's *Declaration and Address*, we recognize that this document, written in a much earlier time, is anything but antiquated. Perhaps now more than ever the clarion call for unity among God's people connects with a culture frustrated with division, hatred, and war.

The Church of the Holy Sepulcher in Jerusalem contains the traditional sites of Jesus' death and burial. Amidst all the ornate mosaics, candles, incense, and paintings, I noticed an historic display of another kind. In one section of the large multiplex of chapels and cathedrals the Coptic Church holds its services. In another area the Greek Orthodox gather to worship. In yet a third area the Roman Catholic Church meets for prayer and meditation. In all, six different Christian bodies maintain control of separate chapels and shrines. At first this might appear to be a beautiful mosaic of God's people working together under one roof. This is far from the truth, however. In actuality, the various Christian orders maintain their *own* space exclusively and rarely interact with one another. The *dis*unity is so stark, in fact, that a Muslim family actually controls the keys to the basilica and unlocks and locks it every day under the watchful eye of three clerics of the main branches of Christianity!

This display is repeated a thousand times the world over. What is seen in the Church of the Holy Sepulcher is a microcosm of what happens worldwide when we allow our differences rather than our similarities to define us. American Protestant Christianity is no different. One group criticizes another. Labels and lists dominate our perceptions of who is "in" and who is "out." Even within the heritage of the Stone-Campbell tradition, we are quick to "denominate" those who are different from us, pointing out their faults while becoming defensive when others point out our own.

In many respects the religious climate of early nineteenth-century America is similar to that of today. Denominations continue to multiply (or "split"), church leaders major in the minors, congregations become territorial, and all of this occurs while millions of people live far from the kingdom of God. Truly, Thomas Campbell's propositions from 1809 need to be revisited and reapplied for this new millennium.

Unity Is Not Optional

We need to hear Thomas Campbell's first proposition as a straight arrow shot into the darkness of division: "That the church of Christ upon earth is essentially, intentionally, and constitutionally one". The New Testament Church knew plenty about factions and splits (e.g. 1 Corinthians 1:10-12), but her nature still reflected the oneness of Christ himself. Jesus Christ cannot be divided (1 Corinthians 1:13), and we are his body, thus, by definition, united. My hand may be severed from my body, but apart from the connection with my body my hand has no life. I may be severed from my spiritual body (the church), but apart from my connection with the body of Christ I have no life.

Jesus is the Vine and we are the branches (John 15). If we are connected to the Vine, we are, by default, connected to other branches. This relationship is not optional. It is our nature. It is who we are.

I have a sister, and at some point she may choose to disown me. However, even though she may not *treat* me as her brother anymore, I am still biologically her brother. She cannot "unmake" me from being her brother. Therefore, as Campbell says, "There ought to be no schisms, no uncharitable divisions among them" (Prop. 2).

A couple expressed their unhappiness over the way they were treated by others in our church—unfairly as they saw it. If this couple leaves, our prayer is that they will remain connected to the body of Christ even if it is not with us, because unity is not an option. Unfortunately, there are countless situations similar to this one. While this reality exists and will continue to exist until Jesus returns, we also have the reality of the oneness of the body of Christ. It is because of *this* reality that there ought to be no schisms or uncharitable divisions among us.

If I slice an apple pie into eight pieces and serve my guests, no one gives a second thought to the *dis*unity of that pie. It was not made for unity but for division. It was made to be eaten! But the church was not created to be severed or divided. Jesus is the head of *one* body. Thus, when we are divided it should cause us great consternation and pain;

for this which has happened should not be. It goes against our nature and identity.

A Cause for Division

So what has brought us to such division? As Thomas Campbell rightly points out, many of our church schisms come because of hermeneutics—ways of understanding or interpreting scripture. Campbell acknowledges that Christians will come to differing interpretations of the New Testament, but he clearly and accurately writes that "inferences and deductions from scripture...are not formally binding upon the consciences of Christians farther than they perceive the connection, and evidently see that they are so" (Prop. 6).

How many interpretations are there filling books with inferences and deductions from scripture that churches have allowed to become formally binding upon Christians? The list would go on indefinitely. Views of the end times, how communion is served, debt vs. no debt, church buildings vs. house churches, and opinions concerning Halloween are only a few examples that readily come to mind. People left one church because the children's ministry had an Easter egg hunt (let alone the fact that they used the term "Easter" instead of "Resurrection Sunday").

Some of our church divisions come through "partial neglect of the expressly revealed will of God," and some of our divisions come through "human opinions and human inventions" (Prop. 11). Either way, Campbell points out, these "have been the immediate, obvious and universally acknowledged causes of all the corruptions and divisions that ever have taken place in the church of God" (Prop. 11).

Room for Opinions

Many churches hold to various "litmus tests" for full acceptance into the social network of the church. Certainly churches should have biblical standards for membership, and they should take seriously the call to "make disciples" not decisions. But what happens too many times is that, although people understand the standards for "formal" membership in a church, the more important issue may be the *informal* membership standards. How does one *really* connect with people in a congregation?

A person may be a baptized (immersed) believer in Jesus Christ, but some believe that if at the person's baptism the words, "For the forgiveness of sins and to receive the gift of the Holy Spirit," were not uttered it invalidates the baptismal experience. Communion may be a central part of a worship service but if the "words of institution" are not used, that church is deemed liberal or too "free." Someone desires to connect with a local church, but he let it slip in a conversation with an elder that he was taught that once you're saved, you're always saved, and the person is quickly ushered out the back door. Another individual comes to a church and happens to mention—not knowing that this has been a major bone of contention among some folks—that she believes in

> "UNITE IN
> THE BONDS
> OF AN ENTIRE
> CHRISTIAN
> UNITY"

the Rapture, and her welcome is short lived. These are but a few examples of litmus tests used by churches, usually by informal means.

Perhaps speaking to matters such as these, Campbell writes that "it is not necessary that persons should have a particular knowledge or distinct apprehension of all divinely revealed truths in order to entitle them to a place in the church" (Prop. 8). In other words, not everyone is going to come to the same conclusions concerning eschatology, pneumatology, or ecclesiology. Just because someone may have been taught a different view of the end times, will that exclude him or her from being in communion with us? Granted, there are biblical truths that are essential to what it means to be a Christ follower, but that list is much shorter than what many churches and Christians make it out to be.

The Essentials

One of the beauties of our Movement is that we agreed to unite around the essentials of the faith, allow opinions in non-essential matters, and attempt to demonstrate love in all things. So what are the essentials?

A wise preacher told me one time that there is only one essential—Jesus Christ, crucified and raised. Out of this "essential," we respond in faith to a number of important biblical truths such as baptism, confession, our walk in the Spirit, and so forth. But there are only two ways we can go in life: toward Jesus or away from him. If we're moving toward Jesus, then even if we don't have everything figured out yet, including baptism, we at least are humbling ourselves and will come to greater understandings as we walk with him. Is this not what happened to Thomas and Alexander Campbell themselves concerning baptism? Were they not Christ followers before they came to the conviction that they needed to be immersed?

As we continue in the twenty-first century, those of us in the Stone-Campbell heritage need to place less emphasis on judging who is "saved" and who is not "saved," and spend more time lifting up Jesus Christ. It is not my job to make everyone believe what I believe about baptism, the Lord's Supper, the Holy Spirit, etc. But it is my job to love them as Jesus loves them and to lift him up so that he will draw all people to himself.

Moving Forward

Our plea for unity is not a naïve belief that all people will exegete scripture the same way for all times. Nor is this a denial that the Bible communicates clearly on matters of the faith (for example, that Jesus Christ died for our sins, was buried and rose againq1). Our plea for unity is based on a conviction "that division among Christians is a horrid evil, fraught with many evils. It is anti-Christian, as it destroys the visible unity of the body of Christ; as if he were divided against himself" (Prop. 10).

In the aftermath of Hurricane Katrina in New Orleans in 2005, Journey Christian Church started a non-denominational ministry to help people rebuild their lives after the storm. It was intentionally opened to believers from all traditions, praying that God would use this ministry as a means to express the oneness of his people. A piece of land owned by a church in a particular denomination was donated to another congregation in that same denomination. The minister of that church called and said, "Great news! This land has been given to us, so why don't we work together to build a community center through this non-denominational ministry?" We both believed this could be the start of a great movement of unity as we served broken and hurting people together.

> "ENCOURAGE THE PEOPLE TO GO FORWARD UPON THE FIRM GROUND OF OBVIOUS TRUTH"

Once the property was being transferred, however, this minister's board intervened and said the property could only be used by their denomination for the purposes of their denomination. Although we continue to help one another and we have maintained a good friendship, we were saddened that two churches from different backgrounds were not able to work together in a more tangible way for the kingdom of God.

When we see our primary identity not as being part of a denomination but the kingdom of God, we are in a much better position to welcome people from different traditions than if we have to uphold our own denomination as a test of fellowship. There are numerous examples of how churches across denominational lines have served together, and we have experienced that in varying degrees in New Orleans, but we are reminded of the great work for unity which still needs to be done.

So how do we move forward from here? What can we learn from the *Declaration and Address* that can help us in our new millennium? First and foremost, we affirm that unity is not optional. Oneness in the body of Christ is essential. Simply put: it is who we are even though we do not always act that way.

Second, we recognize how we have contributed to divisiveness and sectarianism within our own context of ministry. Churches are built on relationships—relationship with Jesus Christ and one another. When relationships are severed, people leave churches. On a larger scale, when relationships are severed, not only do churches split but entire denominations split. This is an oversimplification of how division occurs but it gets at the practical matter of how we fail at times to heal broken relationships, ask for forgiveness, and forgive others.

Third, we become intentional at bridge building. The very fact that Thomas Campbell wrote the *Declaration and Address* indicates that he wanted to *do* something about the disunity of his day. It is far too easy for us to slip into the convenience and comfortable posturing of accepting division with an attitude of "that's just the way it is." Thomas Campbell chose not to accept division. He resisted this and recognized that the best remedy for division is to focus on unity. We will always have areas in which we disagree (non-essentials), and we should have freedom to express our ideas and discuss these matters. But these discussions should come under the broader commitment of unity on the core matter of faith—our commitment to Jesus Christ.

Finally, we remember our commitment that in all things we are to love one another. As the scripture says, "Above all, love each other deeply, because love covers over a multitude of sins" (1 Peter 4:8). The Apostle John reminds us, "Dear friends, let us love one another, for love comes from God. Everyone who loves has been born of God and knows God. Whoever does not love does not know God, because God is love" (1 John 4:7-8).

Love born from God does not wink at sin or overlook truth but always seeks God's kingdom first and strives for others to be reconciled through Jesus Christ. Our Movement, the Stone-Campbell *Restoration* Movement, seeks to restore not simply biblical doctrine but the biblical action of laying down our lives for one another. What is love? "This is how we know what love is: Jesus Christ laid down his life for us. And we ought to lay down our lives for one another" (1 John 3:16, NRSV).

Biblical truth does not separate doctrine from practice. If we claim to know God, then we will demonstrate that in the way we treat one another. For the Stone-Campbell Movement to continue moving forward in the twenty-first century, our churches and believers need to wed our *understanding* of truth with the *Spirit* of truth. Our world is ripe for the harvest. Now, more than ever, the message of the *Declaration and Address* needs to ring out loud and clear that Jesus is Lord and that he calls us to be one in order to reach our lost and broken world.

"Simple Evangelical Christianity" for a New Frontier

Daniel A. Rodriquez

In 1809, from their meeting place in Western Pennsylvania, the Christian Association of Washington, with its spokesperson Thomas Campbell, stood near the edge of the Northwest Territory—those lands east of the Mississippi River, and between the Ohio River and the Great Lakes. Ultimately, this territory was organized into the present states of Ohio (1803), Indiana (1816), Illinois (1818), Michigan (1837) and Wisconsin (1848). But in 1809, the Northwest Territory and the land farther west known as the Louisiana Purchase (1803) represented the promise of almost limitless westward expansion, prosperity, and divine blessings on the New World. Pioneers traveling through Western Pennsylvania were flooding into the Northwest Territory and even beyond the Mississippi to pursue the fledgling "American Dream."

Would the ministers of the gospel of Christ who were accompanying the settlers into these new frontiers promote the seemingly endless denominational and sectarian divisions that plagued the original colonies and the Old World from which many had recently come? Were the settlements in these new territories to become the breeding ground for further divisions among those who call Jesus "Lord"? Or, as Thomas Campbell and his colleagues hoped, would the frontier become the fertile context where Christ's church would "resume her original constitutional unity and purity, and thus be exalted to the enjoyment of her promised prosperity—that the Jews may be speedily converted, and the fullness of the gentiles brought in" (*Declaration and Address* 22:33-35)? It would behoove Christians in the young republic not to fail to recognize the mission opportunity that lay ahead. The "auspicious phenomena of the times" did not escape the notice of Thomas Campbell:

> "MANIFESTING TO EACH OTHER THEIR MUTUAL CHARITY, AND ZEAL FOR THE TRUTH"

> Can the Lord expect, or require, any thing less, from a people in such unhampered circumstances—from a people so liberally furnished with all means and mercies, than a thorough reformation, in all things civil and religious, according to his word?" (8:10-14).

> Dearly beloved brethren, why should we deem it a thing incredible, that the church of Christ, in this highly favored country should resume that original unity, peace and purity, which belongs to its constitution and constitutes its glory? (10:16-19).

In 2009, the two-hundredth anniversary of the publication of the *Declaration and Address*, do we appreciate the "auspicious phenomena of the times"? We too stand on the edge of a new frontier, the unprecedented expansion of the Christian faith into what missiologists commonly refer to as the "10/40 Window," where the vast majority of the world's "un-reached people" live. This rectangular-shaped window extends from West Africa to East Asia, from ten degrees north to forty degrees north of the equator. The 10/40 Window is also referred to as "The Resistant Belt" because it encompasses the majority of the world's Muslims, Hindus, and Buddhists.

Led not only by Western missionaries, but increasingly by indigenous leaders from Africa, Latin America, and Asia, Christians are trying to establish beachheads of what Thomas Campbell referred to as "simple evangelical Christianity" (4:13, 17) on the "new frontier of Christian mission." They too recognize the critical need for Christian unity. Motivated by a desire to participate in the *Missio Dei* (Latin for "God's mission"), the ecumenical gatherings and documents associated with the Lausanne Movement (http://www.lausanne.org/) are especially noteworthy for those of us inspired by the Christian Association of Washington and *The Declaration and Address*. In 1974, 2,300 evangelical leaders from 150 countries gathered in Switzerland to pledge themselves "to seek a deeper unity in truth, worship, holiness and mission." Concerning the latter, they recognized that "Evangelism also summons us to unity, because our oneness strengthens our witness, just as our disunity undermines our gospel of reconciliation" (*Lausanne Covenant* 1974, Paragraph 7). Conveners and participants in the ecumenical gatherings of Christians in Lausanne (1974), Pattaya (1980), Manila (1989), Thailand (2004), and soon in Cape Town (2010), represent contemporary efforts to "restore unity, peace and purity" based upon the "Divine Standard" for the purpose of a greater missionary harvest inspired by the glorious throne scene described by John:

> After this I looked, and there was a great multitude that no one could count, from every nation, from all tribes and peoples and languages, standing before the throne and before the Lamb, robed in white, with palm branches in their hands. They cried out in a loud voice, saying, "Salvation belongs to our God who is seated on the throne, and to the Lamb!" (Rev. 7:9-10, NRSV)

Gatherings such as those associated with the Lausanne Movement reflect the conviction of Thomas Campbell who later in life lamented to his son Alexander that the "movement" would progress still more "if the public advocates from the pulpit and the press would only keep their temper, use soft words and hard arguments" (quoted by J.H. Garrison in *The Story of a Century*, 1909, 30). Unfortunately, we have too often ignored Campbell's advice to those committed to restoring New Testament Christianity. He observed: "Till you associate, consult and advise together; and in a friendly and Christian manner explore the subject [of unity], nothing can be done" (14:6-7). Certainly one of the "auspicious phenomena" of our time is the historic opportunity for "hearty and zealous co-operation to promote the unity, purity and prosperity of [Christ's] church" (15:45) with other Christians, especially those from the so-called "Majority World" (formerly referred to as the "Third World" and "Two-Thirds World").

One of the potential and positive outcomes from such "friendly" associations, conversations, and cooperation with non-Western believers, including ethnic minorities in the United States, will certainly be an appreciation for the role of our respective socio-historical and socio-economic contexts upon our reading and interpretation of the Bible. Such "friendly" associations and conversations will help us realize that there is an excellent epistemological rationale for concurring with Campbell that our commitment is to the Bible and not to any human interpretation of the Scriptures:

> Ye believe that the word itself ought to be our rule and not any human explication of it; so do we. Ye believe that no man has a right to judge, to exclude, or reject, his professing Christian brother; except in so far as he stands condemned, or rejected, by the express letter of the law: —so do we. Ye believe that the great fundamental law of unity and love ought not to be violated to make way for exalting human opinions to an equality with express revelation, by making them articles of faith and terms of communion—so do we." (21:13-21)

Recent works by scholars like Samuel Escobar and Philip Jenkins, including *The New Global Mission: The Gospel from Everywhere to Everyone (Christian Doctrine in Global Perspective)*, *The Next Christendom: The Coming of Global Christianity*, and most recently, *The New Faces of Christianity: Believing the Bible in the Global South*, illustrate how our readings of the Bible, like those of Africans, Asians, Latin Americans, and those of minority groups here in the United States, are informed unconsciously, if not consciously, by our *Sitz en Liben* (i.e., historical context), including such seemingly benign characteristics as our gender, ethnic or racial identity, religious and political affiliations and convictions, socio-economic status, and even our sexual orientation. These additional "lenses" or filters tend to bias our reading and interpretation of the Scriptures in favor of what is in our own best interest.

Here lies an additional reason for not binding "inferences and deductions from scripture premises...upon the consciences of Christians further than they perceive the connection" (Prop. 6). Campbell made an important distinction between "what is expressly enjoined by the authority of our Lord Jesus Christ and his Apostles upon the New Testament church; either in express terms, or by approved precedent" (Prop. 3), and between doctrines and practices deduced from "inferences" based upon "human reasoning." Perhaps Campbell was aware of the "subjective" nature of human inferences and deductions. Whether he was aware of what might be referred to as the "impossibility of objectivity" when approaching the biblical text or not, today's biblical scholars and social scientists have made us aware that it is not just Majority World, feminist or liberation theologians who read and interpret the Bible contextually. Even white, middle-class males who are ministers of non-instrumental Churches of Christ in Tennessee or Alabama read the Bible through extra-biblical lenses or filters that often unconsciously enable them to uphold the status quo and thereby protect their vested interests. Recall that 150 years ago unconscious contextual filters enabled many sincere Bible-believing members of churches associated with the Restoration Movement to conclude that slavery as practiced in *antebellum* America was a divinely sanctioned institution.

If we will "associate, consult and advise together...in a friendly and Christian manner" with those Christians who seek to glorify the God of our Lord Jesus Christ, as Campbell advised, we will certainly become aware of other dimensions of God's kingdom that are hidden from us due to our contextual biases. For instance, we will discover that there are others who have sought and continue to seek to restore New Testament Christianity. But rather than focusing on first-century patterns and practices of corporate worship or church governance, they focus on the calls to personal piety and love for enemy as well as friend found in the explicit commands of Christ (cf. Mark 12: 31; John 13:34-35) and approved precedent of the Apostles and the early church (cf. Acts 2:24-47; 4:32-37; 11:27-30). Still others focus on restoring the evangelistic zeal and focus of the first-century church or the charismatic nature of the church described in the Acts, Romans, and the Corinthian correspondence.

> "ASSOCIATE, CONSULT AND ADVISE TOGETHER...IN A FRIENDLY AND CHRISTIAN MANNER"

What contextual factors cause some truth-seekers to focus on patterns of worship, while others focus on personal holiness, and still others on evangelism or the role of the Holy Spirit? We need not conjecture as to the contextual source of their biases or spiritual blind spots. Instead, let us "associate, consult and advise together; and in a friendly and Christian manner" enable one another to share the unique perspective that the Holy Spirit has opened up to each of us. Let us humbly recognizing that we are all gazing intently at the same scene, but from different vantage points, which opens our eyes to certain salient features of biblical Christianity, but blind us to others.

A healthy dose of humility when declaring "thus saith the Lord" is long overdue among many who embrace the restoration vision associated with the *Declaration and Address*. Why not also confess, like the Apostle Paul, our inherent limitation: "For now we see in a mirror, dimly, but then we will see face to face. Now I know only in part; then I will know fully, even as I have been fully known"? (1 Cor. 13:12). Why not acknowledge, like Paul that if we truly desire to restore New Testament Christianity, there is something more important than restoring patterns of worship, church discipline, or structures of church governance? There is something more elusive to which we should commit ourselves: to imitate the love of our Savior toward our enemies as well as our neighbors and friends (John 13:34-35). His love for his disciples enabled the Lord to forgive their lack of faith, their disloyalty, and even their disobedience to his explicit commands.

Consider the following example. In Acts 11:1-3 the apostles criticize Peter for sharing the gospel and table fellowship with Cornelius and his household because they were uncircumcised Gentiles. After hearing Peter's defense (verses 4-17), the church's most influential leaders finally acquiesced. "When they heard this, they were silenced. And they praised God, saying, 'Then God has given even to the Gentiles the repentance that leads to life'" (Acts 11:18).

Jesus had stated explicitly, "Go therefore and make disciples of all nations, baptizing them in the name of the Father and of the Son and of the Holy Spirit, and teaching them to obey everything that I have commanded you" (Matt. 28:19, *NRSV*). Their racial prejudices and ethnocentrism had clearly blinded the apostles and elders of the church in Jerusalem to the meaning of Christ's explicit command. In spite of their disobedience and spiritual blindness, however, the Lord was patient with them and their incorrect interpretation of his mission mandate to be his "witnesses in Jerusalem, in all Judea and Samaria, and to the ends of the earth" (Acts 1:8). This episode alone should humble us, as we consider the possibility that we too are "spiritually blinded" by our prejudices and biases to the true meaning of at least some explicit commands of the Lord.

In our clarion call to restore biblical unity in the twenty-first century, we must not only invite others to learn from us, we must also humbly ask them to teach us "the Way of God more accurately." Perhaps this kind of humility when associating, consulting, and advising together with "our brethren from all denominations" (a favorite phrase of Campbell) would nurture the friendly and Christian manner of exploring the subject of unity that has consumed much of our rhetoric and energies during the past two hundred years.

One more related observation from the *Declaration and Address* stands out to me on the eve of that historic document's bicentennial:

the understated "means" of restoring the unity of the Christian church.
Repeatedly in the *Declaration and Address*, Campbell recognized that,
ultimately, restoring the church's "consti-
tutional unity" (11:1) would require divine

**"THE DUTY THEN IS
OURS; BUT EVENTS
BELONG TO GOD"**

aid. Humans, through their weakness and
prejudice, are often blind to the will of God.
Unfortunately, a contentious public debate
or blistering verbal critique in a divisive publication will seldom if ever "open their eyes."
Instead, Campbell urged his readers to listen to the divinely inspired
advice given to Timothy:

> And the Lord's servant must not be quarrelsome but kindly to
> everyone, an apt teacher, patient, correcting opponents with
> gentleness. God may perhaps grant that they will repent and
> come to know the truth, and that they may escape from the
> snare of the devil, having been held captive by him to do his will
> (2 Tim. 2:24-26, NRSV).

Several times in the *Declaration and Address*, Campbell echoes the
apostle's often forgotten words when he says, "The duty then is ours;
events belong to God" (11:35). He speaks of the reliance upon God
that should characterize our associations with those who understand,
embrace, and teach the divine will differently than he and his colleagues
in the Christian Association of Washington:

But if any of our dear brethren ["of all denominations," 10:7, 11:7], from whom we should expect better things, should through weakness or prejudice, be in any thing otherwise minded, than we have ventured to suppose; we charitably hope, that, in due time, God will reveal even this to them:—Only let such, neither refuse to come to the light; nor yet, through prejudice, reject it, when it shines upon them." (21:25-31)

May the Lord soon open the eyes of his people to see these things in their true light; and excite them to come up out of their wilderness condition—out of this Babel of confusion—leaning upon their beloved, and embracing each other in him; holding fast the unity of the spirit in the bond of peace. (23:20-24)

Clearly, Thomas Campbell and his colleagues in the Christian Association of Washington recognized that the centuries-old disagreements that divide the historic Christian church must be settled not by contentious public criticism and divisive debates, but rather by friendly and humble association and cooperation with our brothers and sisters "from all denominations." Even more importantly, like their Savior in John 17, Campbell and his colleagues recognized that the sovereign God must mercifully intercede to bring about unity. Unity would require that God "open the eyes of his people" who are in "anything otherwise minded." In the meantime his people are to hold fast the unity of the Spirit in the bond of peace.

So on the eve of the two-hundredth anniversary of the 1809 *Declaration and Address,* we must pray as did its author, Thomas Campbell: "May the good Lord subdue the corruptions and heal the divisions of his people. Amen and amen" (Appendix, 39:34).

From a series of stained glass windows depicting Unity and Liberty in Christ in Nashville's Thomas W. Phillips Memorial Building, this medallion shows Thomas Campbell in the "upper room" of the Pennsylvania farmhouse writing his testament of unity. Highly symbolic, the original design was created by Gus Baker and executed in glass by L. L. Morris, c. 1958.

Things We Surely Believe

Amy Lignitz Harken

These are frustrating times for people of faith.

A member of my congregation teaches biology at a Catholic university perched just a few miles from the Kansas-Missouri border. The Kansas State Board of Education wrestles quite frequently and famously with the issues of creationism and evolution. Just this year, Missouri voters wrestled with a proposal to restrict use of stem-cell research in the state. You can imagine the water cooler conversations at that university, especially among the Protestant scientists.

My friend frequently attends lectures delivered by visiting scholars. Some lectures leave her glowing with affirmation of the peaceable coexistence within herself of a deep appreciation of human intellect, and a deep faith that all that is knowable and discoverable by the human mind is part of God's good creation. Other lectures, however, leave her fuming. Take, for instance, the lecture in which the speaker discussed the beliefs of different churches. Some denominations believe the right way, some believe the wrong way, and some, intoned the lecturer, "don't know what they believe, like the Disciples of Christ."

Ouch.

As I flinch from that barb, I suspect that it stings as it does because it carries a bit of truth. Two centuries ago Thomas Campbell wrote that "nothing ought to be inculcated upon Christians as articles of faith, nor required of them as terms of communion, but what is expressly taught and enjoined upon them in the word of God." I wonder whether, in writing that, Campbell inadvertently caused what would become the Christian Church (Disciples of Christ) to shy so far away from making definitive belief statements that we have abandoned expressing our beliefs altogether.

Even worse, I wonder whether in trying to be "relevant" (or inoffensive) within secular culture, we have abandoned, become ashamed of, or even determined to be untrue to the hard things of our faith such as sin, repentance, salvation, and even miracles. Has our strident congregational autonomy left us afraid even to broach the subject of just what we do believe as a denomination? Or, if we are able to articulate what distinguishes our denomination, can we only talk about *how* we do things (we invite everyone to participate in the Lord's Supper), rather than *why* we do them that way (because the Bible tells us that's the way Jesus would want it). I wonder whether Campbell's harsh statements about "human opinions and the inventions of men," and his blaming divisions among Christians on "the imposing of our private opinions upon each other" implanted in our denominational DNA an inclination to shun tradition altogether. If that's the case, have we devalued our own history?

The fact is, as the Christian Church (Disciples of Christ), we do have particular beliefs, the roots of which reach deep into a rich and fertile soil of tradition, scripture, history, and theological reflection. Moreover, these beliefs yield fruit today that could provide sustenance to many of God's people who hunger for a faith that is authentic and alive, and does not ask anyone to set aside his or her intelligence. The two-hundredth anniversary of Campbell's *Declaration and Address* is a fitting occasion to consider our denominational beliefs and practices and to celebrate them, not as something that makes us better than, or even different from, our brothers and sisters of other denominations, but as a place to get our footing so we may reach out in honesty, love, purpose, and, ultimately, in the Christian unity Campbell so earnestly sought.

If I imagine my friend giving in to her temptation to stand up in the middle of that lecture hall to make a bold defense, I imagine she would have started with the Lord's Supper. (It particularly chaps her hide that she is not allowed to take communion at "ecumenical" campus masses.) She could have said, "We believe that scripture tells us that every time we come together in the name of Jesus to worship, we celebrate the Lord's Supper. But as Disciples of Christ, we believe that the table is open to everyone." And what do we mean that our table is open? We need not be prideful or defensive, although we may recall times when we have been made unwelcome at a communion table, or when others, eyebrows raised, declined communion from the hand of our minister, our elder, or our neighbor in the pew. The hospitality we believe Jesus calls us to extend at the table is only a part of our belief.

Our open table means that every person is invited because Jesus welcomed and invited everyone to be a full participant in the kingdom of

God. This includes the poor, and the poor in spirit. So when we say our table is open, we are reminded of the impoverished across the ocean, as well as those suffering from mental illness across the street. Our open table means there is enough to go around. At our open table, we remember that Jesus welcomed all to the kingdom, including those who had a shady past. So at the table we are reminded of our own shady past, and know we are among those who have fallen short of the glory of God. Our open table means we understand that the fallen, the weak, and the sinful need the gifts of the table the most. And when we hear the words of Jesus that his cup is poured out for forgiveness, we know that we need forgiveness and that we find our perfection, not in what we do, but in what God does.

> "THE LORD'S SUPPER... THAT GREAT ORDINANCE OF UNITY AND LOVE"

Our open table also says that one need not be ordained to serve from it. One need not be ordained to utter the words of Jesus that instituted the celebration. One need not be ordained, or licensed—or for that matter even very nice—to serve from a plate or a tray holding the bread, or a chalice or a tray holding little plastic cups containing the fruit of the vine. As the priesthood of all believers, we need only understand that we are bound to each other through Christ, and that we are bound to Christ with each other. So, we are bound to the sinners and the saints. We are bound to the hungry and to the self-indulgent, to the creditor and the debtor, to the oppressed and the oppressor, to the stingy and the generous. Our open table means we are part of each other, that we need each other, just as we need Jesus.

I believe, as a denomination, we can say we believe that.

My friend could have continued with the sacraments, saying we practice "believer's baptism" by full immersion. She could have explained that while we recognize and affirm the practices of "sprinkling" and of baptizing infants, we believe the Bible generally shows people to be baptized when they come to believe Jesus is the Christ, and make a confession of that belief. Further, we understand that biblical examples of baptism demonstrate full immersion.

But what do we mean by "believer's" baptism? We mean that by calling ourselves "Christian," we believe something very specific about our relationship with God. We believe that it is not simply a matter of "being good" or "doing good" because such gives us a good feeling. We believe that God's love for us is so astoundingly deep, as revealed to the world in the person of Jesus of Nazareth, that we strive to be generous and merciful, forbearing and hopeful, even when it *doesn't* feel good. In our believer's baptism, we acknowledge that our assent to the promises God has for us involves something in addition to whatever spiritual euphoria may grasp us from time to time. We assent that we love God not only with all our heart and soul and strength, but with all our mind as well. We assent with our hearts *and* our minds to the foolishness of the cross, even as we try to grasp its meaning. And we assent that living a life of faith means study, and consideration, and that we—not our preacher, not our parents, not our church—bear responsibility for our relationship with God.

Our believer's baptism means we make ourselves part of a community of other believers, where we can come to know God better through witnessing, accountability, and even disagreement with each other.

And, while we may or may not say we were "born again," our believer's baptism is an outward sign that we have said "Yes!" to God's power to effect a transformation in the depths of our hearts that is palpable and radical, significant and permanent. We believe in this power and we desire this transformation, whether it happens as we rise dripping from the water, or at another time altogether. We believe that God will continue to make our life new as long as we live, and that God can bring the same newness of life in the heart of even our most heinous foe.

Cannot we, as a denomination, say we believe that?

Surely any statement of our beliefs must include (if only to account for) the aphorism our founders insistently handed to us: "No creed but Christ." With all respect to those denominations that include creedal statements as part of worship today, it is worth explaining that, two centuries ago, our founders believed such statements to be sources of division, while Jesus' deep desire was that all who call him Lord be one.

But what does our "no creed" view mean for Disciples today? It means that we believe our faith is a vibrant, growing thing that defies capture or even characterization in a sentence, paragraph, or entire page. We believe that as we study, pray, and exercise our faith, it evolves and causes us to evolve. All that we come to believe and know about God cannot be summed up in a book or a library of books, and even that would be but a sliver of the reality of the divine.

At the same time, each of us does bear responsibility for articulating our faith. So, we are left to tell our own stories. It is our good fortune, however, that our faith finds expression in the glimpses of God we see all around us, in the cities and towns, in the countryside, in the wilderness, in our homes. Our faith is nourished and finds meaning in the small miracles of our daily existence, the ordinary turning from bad to good, from hatred to love, from intolerance to forbearance. We believe that through even the smallest incident, the Holy Spirit can breathe through us, opening worlds of insight into our place in God's kingdom. We understand that the turning of the church calendar affords us many opportunities to state our faith, from Christmas's incarnational declaration "He was born!" to Easter's resurrection shout, "He is risen!" We understand that our statements are made not only with our lips, but with our feet as we stand and walk in the way of justice, and with our hands as we serve our neighbor.

And surely we must complete the famous "No creed but Christ," with its complement, "No book but the Bible," noting the centrality of scripture to the Disciples of Christ. But what does "centrality of scripture" mean? After all, for many Disciples, like my friend, the Bible is something to be studied and revered, yet at the same time the relevance of entire portions seems dubious at best.

The centrality of scripture to our faith means we believe the Bible is the inspired word of God, and its relevance lies in our belief that the God of Abraham, Isaac, and Jacob is our God, too. We believe that the God of Adam and Moses, Eve and Miriam, is our God, too. We believe that the God of Jesus is our God, too. We believe the God of Mary and Mary, of John and John, of Paul, Peter and Priscilla, of Lydia and James, is our God, too. And God's word to them is and always will be the word of our God. The centrality of scripture to our faith means that we understand it to be the best witness available to the life and ministry of the one we call Savior.

The centrality of scripture to our faith means we believe the Bible is a document written by, about, and for human beings, and as such imposes a responsibility upon those who seek inspiration in its pages. The centrality of scripture to our faith means we take it seriously enough to approach our Bibles as books to be studied and considered thoughtfully, and to be allowed to live in a context larger than finite words on a page. It means we have the right to seek its meaning not only in light of the lives and times of those who wrote it, but in light of our own life and time. We believe that each of us comes to scripture with our own experience and expectations, and that our most fruitful reflection often happens when we gather with each other to share and to learn from its pages.

And lest we consign Campbell's hope for a return to the New Testament "primitive" church to the ash bin of the naïve and old-fashioned, the centrality of scripture to our faith means we unleash our imaginations to grasp the implications of the Bible's vision for humanity. Along with Campbell, we consider the powerful movement of the Holy Spirit among those generous, evangelical societies. As we do so, we hear it call to us from beyond our present culture, which tends to isolate us and lies to us that ultimate fulfillment comes with personal prosperity.

In a world where so many human connections involve electronic devices, satellites, and frequent anonymity, the Bible calls us to flesh-and-blood community where we look in each other's eyes, hold each other's hands, and call each other by names given us at birth. In a world that touts personal wealth, the Bible calls us to share so that none have need. In a world that values a good time above all else, the Bible calls us to live in joy. While the world congratulates itself that its young adults are optimistic for personal success, the Bible establishes an expectation for the kingdom of God for everyone. While the world threatens loneliness and exile for those who aren't in the right group, the Bible shows us the power of the passion of a struggling minority. The Bible's vision is far more difficult to achieve than the vision peddled through popular media, but it is real and we believe it is manna for a world that is desperately hungry for something real.

"UNITED
WE SHALL
PREVAIL"

Surely we, as a denomination, believe that.

But the logical question follows: Couldn't we do all that without the institution of "church?" As human institutions, churches certainly are fraught with the same politics, prejudices, power plays, cliques, and rivalries that bedevil any human institution. If we were posed that question, would we stumble? Would recollections of cliquishness, small-mindedness, stinginess, laziness, and all the other vagaries of our lesser selves leap from the recesses of decades of accumulated church memories? How many tales has each of us heard, or lived, about disputes, heated arguments, failed attempts at reconciliations, and worship services that were either boring, oppressive, or little more than feel-good pep talks? The historians among us even may recall early Disciples statements about "dissolving into the body of Christ," and Campbell's detailing of the ugliness that marked the churches of his day.

But my confident hope is that, were my friend asked that question, she would recall the Sunday mornings when the sunlight streams in the towering stained glass windows to illuminate the beaming faces of those who have gathered to worship God in a way they couldn't alone. The deep, joyful current of Spirit flowing through Pentecost Sunday, when baptismal candidates share with the congregation their first expressions of belief. The collective guffaw over a malapropism from the pulpit. The collective grief for the stalwart who finally lost his bodily battle to cancer. The tears brought forth in the back pew by "Because He Lives." Hushed, candle-lit sighs of Christmas Eve. Bedside communion offered into trembling hands. Poor neighborhood mothers grateful to clothe their children. What things we can do together that we cannot do alone!

This was Thomas Campbell's hope for Jesus' church. Not so much that congregations be autonomous, but that they respect the others' individuality. Not so much that we shun every conviction as a threat to our freedom, but that we base our convictions in the biblical witness of Jesus. Not that we shrink from making declarations of our faith, but that we understand our declarations as points of departure for a collective journey upon which Christians of every conceivable stripe have embarked. And that by knowing ourselves, we can be known to our fellow travelers, and know them better, too.

As church we can be what the world is not. We can be diverse without being divided. We can be united without being uniform. As church we can do what the world has not done. We can include without being insular. We can accept and affirm without acquiescing that absolutely anything goes. We can open our hearts without closing our minds, and open our minds without closing our hearts. We can accept humility without being humiliated. We can lose ourselves to a higher purpose without falling apart.

For, as church, our center never was ourselves. It was, is, and always will be Jesus of Nazareth, whom we declare—if we never, ever make any other declaration—is the Christ of God, that is, the flesh-and-blood answer to God's love for each of us. When we let this Jesus, this Christ, be the hub around which all else revolves, as Thomas Campbell implored us to do, many of those things that tend to divide dissipate. We find that living amidst difference is a thing of ease, if not joy. We find ourselves part of a magnificent body, made up of different parts, with different functions, complementing, honing, challenging, magnifying, bettering, and letting ourselves be bettered, as the whole body moves toward Christ's vision, "that all be one."

Surely we, the Christian Church (Disciples of Christ), believe that to be true.

The 21ˢᵗ Century Restoration— Will We Join It?

Greg Taylor

The community was surprised when rough and tumble "Spike" Walker converted to Christ at a brush arbor meeting. Spike—my great grandfather—my grandparents and parents were all baptized in Oklahoma and Kansas Churches of Christ.

But in the seventies, about the time I was baptized, a scandal broke out in my family. My uncle and aunt, Rudy and Kathy Taylor, transferred from a Church of Christ to a Christian Church—a painful move because many family members viewed them as leaving The Church.

Rudy's father—my grandfather—then resigned as elder of the church. "He and my mother truly believed I had 'left the truth,'" Rudy said. "And they moved from the community where we all lived because of what they perceived as humiliation. My father was disappointed in me, and I in him for his response. He gave up the greatest responsibility in life because he thought he was no longer qualified as having 'believing children.'"

But something a woman in the Christian Church said to Rudy has always stuck with him: that he ought to be thankful his parents and family cared enough that they would take a stand, even if it was wrongly handled. Rudy says he holds no grudges—just grief for what was lost. "My parents didn't see me baptize our children. It was so sad for me to listen to my children tell their grandparents about being baptized, obviously thinking that would bring a smile and congratulations. Their news was greeted by silence. It always took some parental explaining when we left Grandma's and Grandpa's house," Rudy said.

Many of our families and churches have some explaining to do.

Embracing a New Worldview

The worldview that Churches of Christ have a privileged place above denominations, insider knowledge of scripture, and a unique place in history is flawed. These notions cause or at least contribute to rifts in families and churches like mine. Leaving one Christian church for another Christian church is not the same as leaving Christ or the truth. My uncle and his family were seeking Christ and truth at least as much as my relatives staying in Churches of Christ.

The worldview of my upbringing taught me to suspect and debate the Methodist and Catholic alike, to reject forms of worship unlike ours and in most extreme cases to view anyone outside Churches of Christ as not truly Christian. At times in our history the idea of making converts shifted away from reaching people who did not know Christ to those who worshiped in ways different from us. And we believed convicting others of our views was tantamount to converting them to Christianity.

In spite of this, the stubborn autonomous streak in us has allowed some communities within Churches of Christ to break free from this conceit and become learners again. And though I'm proud of my family and Stone-Campbell heritage, I want to see our movement grow into a new future faith—one that drinks from wells dug by our faithful fathers and mothers, digs new wells, and questions stagnant thinking of the past and today.

> "MAY THE LORD SOON OPEN THE EYES OF HIS PEOPLE"

This story is personal and risky for me, but this is where I believe new restoration begins: with a change in worldview that brings us to our knees before God and each other, honestly reflecting on our past and imagining a new future.

So my wife and I believe and teach our children that we are part of the larger body of Christ, and that God is much bigger than Churches of Christ and the Stone-Campbell Movement. I know this is no news to many reading this, but I also believe what I'm about to say will challenge all of us in the Stone-Campbell family. We want to fellowship with and participate in the life of Christians worldwide and in various denominations. We want to focus on Christ and why the world cannot live without him, to unite and be faithful to Christ's prayer that we be one (John 17). Living in Uganda and fellowshiping with people of diverse ethnicity, denominations, and politics did more than anything to change my worldview. People with all these differences can and will journey together in Christ. This is not just part of the gospel—it is the result of God's work in Christ and our duty to be faithful participants.

Our worldview is different from that typical of two or three generations of Churches of Christ. For example, my ten-year-old daughter asked, "What's the difference between that Methodist church and ours?" I said there are no differences important enough to explain right now. "Both believe Jesus is God's Son and the Holy Spirit lives in us."

The world is changing and our worldview ought also to change. Rather than asking, "Are the Baptists or the Catholics right?" millions are asking a question on a completely different plane: "Is Jesus the Lord or should I follow Muhammad?" I'm more concerned to tell Muslims and sinners about Jesus than I am debating matters of precise doctrinal formulations with fellow Christians. I'd rather show a wanderer the gospel of Jesus than "convert" an Episcopalian's view of scripture to mine.

Will there be backlash for this attempt to change our worldview? Different tension points for the next generations? Certainly, but we believe in unity and dialogue with Christians across denominations, across the Protestant and Catholic divide. Unity will expand the kingdom of God, help us become missionaries in every land and culture, and bring people to Christ, who teaches that unity and love draw people to himself.

This is already happening. The next generation imagines giving up their lives for Jesus—not with bombs strapped to their chests but with clothes of Christ wrapped around them, in faith that the kingdom we seek penetrates bone and marrow by the sword of the incredible life of Jesus, the God of the universe made flesh once in Christ and again in us.

The New Restoration

A new restoration is rising and is broader than the Stone-Campbell Restoration because it includes Christians from most traditions who are discovering Jesus and the Bible like never before through the power of the Holy Spirit, in house churches and large churches and with tools as varied as Bible translations, the internet, emergent learning communities, and Christian universities.

Restoration language echoes through several overlapping movements that include "Missional," "Emergent," and "Simple Church." This new restoration is making disciples un-tethered to specific denominations but still moored to and fueled by ancient Christianity. They want to break out of the box of modernism and not march to denominational drumbeats. They want to be the hands and feet of Christ in the world.

This new restoration of "simple Christianity" is not simply full of fads and methods but inspires Christians to live at intersections such as Hollywood and Vine and to wonder what would happen if inhabitants of the city set on a hill stepped into the red light district. For example, two ministers decided to start xxxchurch.com to call men out of addiction to pornography and women out of the sex industry. They were criticized by fellow Christians for going to porn trade shows to call people to new life in Christ, but they endured. They have helped tens if not hundreds of thousands of people rise out of sex addictions and have led porn stars to Christ—who says to them "where are your accusers" and "go and sin no more."

A woman decided to start a program for prisoners being released to help them learn not just job skills but how to start their own businesses. A micro-loan helped one man buy a food cart and eventually to purchase two catering trucks.

A Christian rock group is helping with water wells, mosquito nets, education, and training in African countries, which many believe will send more missionaries abroad in the next decade than developed nations such as the United States.

These examples only scratch the surface of a new generation of Christians who, like Jesus, are going to sinners, prisoners, and the poor. For too long I have allowed competition and sectarianism to deter me from cheering on Christians of all kinds worldwide. Jesus said, "I want all of them to be one with each other, just as I am one with you and you are one with me...Then this world's people will know that you sent me. They will know that you love my followers as much as you love me" (John 17:21-23, CEV).

I'm ready to truly live that prayer and let it shape me.

Are we willing to lose our reputations or die to fulfill the prayers of Christ? Am I willing to die for my faith in Jesus Christ, not in war, but in whatever peaceful, radical form that might take in my lifetime? Am I willing to keep agitating for a better world for the poor, for clean water for one billion who have none? Am I willing to keep advocating for peace as long as there is war? As Ghandi said, may we be "the change we wish to see in the world" as we consider how we can join this new restoration of Christians who are living images of Christ in the world.

Will We Join the New Restoration?

Churches of Christ have come to the valley of decision at the foot of a mountain of sectarianism. We have no denominational charter to dissolve, but I believe this is one of those mountains Jesus said a little faith can move. If Churches of Christ continue to believe we occupy a privileged place above Christian history, scripture, and denominations, we dishonor and fail the Stone-Campbell plea for simple Christianity; we're dead on the vine rather than blossoming like a field of wildflowers, Christ's "little ones."

> "IN THIS GLORIOUS CAUSE WE ARE READY TO UNITE WITH YOU"

We're called to unity with all Christians everywhere who call Christ Lord. When Jesus prayed his unity prayer, he didn't parse every doctrine and neither will I here. We live the Christ-life and follow the rule of the Holy Spirit to keep that everlasting covenant God the Father has kept since creation. Christ and Paul and our own more recent forefathers such as Thomas Campbell call us to produce fruit and look for fruit of the Spirit in the lives of fellow disciples.

Will Churches of Christ, Christian Churches/Churches of Christ, and Disciples of Christ join this new restoration? It is not—and never has been—only our restoration, but rather a plea for all Christians everywhere of all times to reunite the family and mutually claim the fact that we've all been adopted and none is the "rightful" heir. But our family can help participants in the new restoration break free from religious molds and live their faith in the marketplace.

I want to see this shift of worldview in Churches of Christ in my lifetime, and I will be "the change I want to see" in the Stone-Campbell Movement and beyond. I will admit I do not stand above other denominations in any way but am a fallible, messed up human being in need daily of immersion in God's life and words, in Jesus' cross and resurrection.

I will admit I have no monopoly on truth or scripture's interpretation. And I will join the great mission of Christ with my fellow disciples, showing my neighbors the good news of Jesus through prayer and words of blessing.

I will follow what I call the "Golden Commission": to preach the gospel as I would have others preach to me—to show a fellow beggar how to get bread.

My uncle Rudy is a newspaper editor and publisher. Every word he writes drips with faith. He says what I want to conclude with:

> I grieve for those who have died without fully knowing the joy I have experienced as a sojourner in Christ. I love the Lord Jesus Christ today because my mother and father taught me, took me to church and lived like Him to the best of their abilities. My highest hope and prayer is that future generations will shed the traditions that separate God's people, and keep the lines of spiritual sharing open for those times when we need to be talking about something more pertinent than what's going on at 17th and Hillside Church. I pray for the day when His body will stand tall, walk straight, extend its arms, wiggle its fingers and toes, flash its eyes and smile broadly,

totally unaware that once its members looked at other body parts as aliens.

A new era is dawning for the Stone-Campbell Movement and a new, larger restoration movement is emerging. Let us join our brothers and sisters in the grand journey of faith in Christ, and in a movement of the Spirit of God that brings us together in ways we never thought possible.

The Problem of Full Communion

Irie L. Session

"When was the first time you realized being a woman was a problem?" Dr. Stacey Floyd-Thomas, Ethicist and Director of Black Church Studies at Brite Divinity School-Texas Christian University, had a way of taking her students places they had never been before. She posed this piercing question to students in her course titled, *African American Women's Literature as a Resource for Womanist Theology.*

The idea of blackness being a problem in American society was nothing new to me. I was all too familiar with the work of W. E. B. Dubois and his treatment of the Negro as a problem. In *Souls of Black Folk*, Dubois probes the tendency of white Americans to skirt around their perception of the Negro as a problem by their use of what he termed "an unasked question":

> Between me and the other world there is ever an unasked question: unasked by some through feelings of delicacy; by others through the difficulty of rightly framing it. All, nevertheless, flutter round it. They approach me in a half-hesitant sort of way, eye me curiously or compassionately, and then, instead of saying directly, How does it feel to be a problem? they say, I know an excellent colored man in my town; or, I fought at

Mechanicsville; or, Do not these Southern outrages make your blood boil? At these I smile, or am interested, or reduce the boiling to a simmer, as the occasion may require. To the real question, How does it feel to be a problem? I answer seldom a word. And yet, being a problem is a strange experience,—peculiar even for one who has never been anything else....[1]

Being black[2] and thought of as a problem was commonplace. However, being thought of as a problem because of my gender was not an idea I had ever considered, at least not until that fall afternoon in seminary. And so I wept.

As I sat in class reflecting on her question, the memories surfaced. I remembered a male church leader reprimanding me with, "The trouble with you women is that you all think you're equal to men." I remembered a minister in Dallas, Texas, sarcastically criticizing my inquisitive nature by remarking, "You were always an 'independent' thinker anyway," and the words of a minister as he explained, "You'll have to leave the Church of Christ to do 'that' kind of ministry." Yes, being black was a problem. But being black, a woman, and a critical thinker with a passion for ministry meant I was more than a problem. I was trouble.

"MUCH DEPENDS UPON YOUR HEARTY ... ENDEAVORS"

While conducting a research project on the Stone-Campbell Movement and its implication for black women in Churches of Christ, I came across another troublesome black female. The young girl was a member of the Church

of Christ some one hundred years after the writing of Thomas Campbell's
Declaration and Address. Her story reveals the imbedded racism and sexism
endemic in the churches of the Stone-Campbell Movement of the time and
exposes how even well-meaning Christians can marginalize segments of society through the misuse of scripture.

In the spring of 1907 a lengthy written exchange appeared in the
Gospel Advocate[3] between two white men, S. E. Harris from the Church of
Christ in Bellwood, Tennessee, and E. A. Elam from Nashville Bible School
in Nashville, Tennessee. The men, both leading members in Churches of
Christ, debated the spiritual, social, and ethical implications of allowing
or disallowing a "colored girl" to worship with whites at the church in
Bellwood. The "colored" girl lived in the household of E.A. Elam and
his wife. It was in the home of the Elams that the young girl first learned
of the gospel message and subsequently became a Christian. So, rather
than attend the nearby Negro church, the Elams brought her to worship
with them in the white congregation. Their rationale for permitting her
to worship with whites was that it would create an opportunity for them
to "teach her and protect her against the sins common to her race."[4]

In a response to Harris's protest that the girl should worship with
her own kind, David Lipscomb, a close friend of the Elams, joined the
written exchange in an attempt to confirm the exemplary handling of
the young girl while living with the Elams:

> As I understand the above case, a Negro child was given Brother
> and Sister Elam to raise. They have carefully raised and trained

her. They have taught her the Bible, carried her to church with them, and she has become a Christian. She is not forward, but deports herself modestly, and is willing to be served last and not participate in the class, which shows she does not thrust herself forward as the social equal of the whites.[5]

Lipscomb held that as long as the young black girl was trained and socialized in a white Christian community, recognized and accepted her own inferior status, wasn't loose or sexually provocative, she was safe from the perceived sin and degradation inherent in her own people—black people—and therefore, posed no threat to white congregants.

Nevertheless, the young girl's presence was causing a "disturbance." She was still viewed as a problem. In fact, Harris writes the following to Elam as a means to communicate the seriousness of the circumstances:

There is a great deal of complaint in the church at this place in regard to the "colored girl" that lives at your house. I simply and kindly take the lead and ask you as a Christian to please, if you think you have any right to, request her to attend the colored church, as it would quiet the disturbance at this place, and, I think, be a great help to the congregation at this place. There are a great many of the members sore over the state of affairs....[6]

The real reason for such an upheaval was that the white parents didn't want the young black girl associating with their children. Unfortunately for this young girl, to whites, being black and female was the embodiment of a threat. Her presence altered something in the atmo-sphere. It caused discomfort and fear. Not unlike many churches in the twenty-first century, the white parents in the church at Bellwood were afraid of and opposed to their children socializing and even worship-ping with blacks in general. However, in their minds, a young black girl created a different set of problems. Their irrational fear took precedence over their faith in the God of both the Jew and Gentile.

Fear of black females is a social and sexual phenomenon having its genesis in the racial stereotype of the black female body as dangerously hypersexual. When Europeans invaded Africa they discovered scantily clad natives and misinterpreted their cultural practices for licentious-ness. The young girl in the church in Bellwood carried the baggage of these racial and sexual stereotypes causing whites to view her as a prob-lem. Black women in the twenty-first century carry similar baggage, and the church through its sexist practices reinforces these stereotypes.

There is a direct connection between the racial and sexual stereotyp-ing of black females and their subjugation in church and society. The *Declaration and Address* can provide a liberating lens through which to view an alternate method for responding to issues of race, sex, and class which can lead to the full communion of all Christians in the kingdom of God.

In the *Declaration and Address* Campbell asserts the following ideals concerning the kingdom of God and full communion:

It is to us, a pleasing consideration that all Churches of Christ which mutually acknowledge each other as such, are not only agreed in the great doctrines of faith and holiness, but are also materially agreed as to the positive ordinances of gospel institution; so that our differences, at most, are about the things in which the kingdom of God does not consist, that is, about matters of private opinion or human convention....But this we do sincerely declare, that there is nothing we have hitherto received as matters of faith or practice which is not expressly taught and enjoined in the word of God, either in express terms or approved precedent, that we would not heartily relinquish, so that we might return to the original constitutional unity of the Christian Church; and, in this happy unity, enjoy full communion with all our brethren, in peace and charity.[7]

As a black woman of faith who was also reared in Churches of Christ, I'm compelled both to ask and answer some pressing questions related to the above quote. For example, "Of what exactly does the kingdom of God consist?" and "How do black Churches of Christ experience *full communion* when women—a segment of that same tradition—are believed to be a problem?"

One of the major social crises of the twenty-first century is sexism. Clearly, sexism is a justice issue for women in general. But for black women it is especially damaging because, along with sexism, black women have the added burden of experiencing the interlocking oppressive systems of racism and classism as well. Yet the exclusivism of Churches of Christ creates within the black church a culture of sexism—

giving its leaders a feeling of both doctrinal and male superiority. Facing the reality of sexism in black Churches of Christ makes it possible for black women in the twenty-first century to connect with the problematic black girl in Bellwood, Tennessee. If the sexist culture in black Churches of Christ is to ever change, black women in Churches of Christ must realize that the same oppressive structures that caused the little black girl in Bellwood, Tennessee, to be "othered" and not be worthy enough even to be named are the same oppressive structures existing in twenty-first-century churches.

> "IN THIS HAPPY UNITY, ENJOY FULL COMMUNION WITH ALL OUR BRETHREN, IN PEACE AND CHARITY."

Thomas Campbell's *Declaration and Address* is a prophetically relevant and urgent message that can address the issue of sexism. Granted, the *Declaration and Address,* like the *Declaration of Independence,* at the time it was penned, didn't have blacks in mind. Nevertheless, upon reflection, the messages of both documents can be a source of liberation and hope for black people. The *Declaration and Address* in its concern for the full communion of believers despite their differences is a message that is both urgent and relevant for the twenty-first-century church. Experiencing full communion implies that those for whom Christ died, those who have accepted Jesus as Lord, are no longer seen as problems. Moreover, the message of full communion speaks to the church's responsibility to address the plight of those whom society says are problems. For example, the homeless, the under-educated, illegal immigrants, social outcasts such as prostitutes, persons living with HIV/AIDS, gays & lesbians, women of color in America, as well as women living in Third World countries, are all groups considered by today's society as problems.

However, the message of full communion creates the picture of a faith community that refuses to promote political, economic, racial, or gender superiority to justify the marginalization of certain groups, but rather one that deliberately and respectfully engages the "other," the "foreigner," and the "outsider" in meaningful dialogue in order to uncover commonalities that foster unity in Christ—an urgent and relevant message for twenty-first-century Christians. Who could argue that many twenty-first-century churches continue to have an inward focus with little or no concern for issues of social justice or unity? We must be relentless in our identification of such ungodly attitudes wherever they exist—especially in the churches of this Stone-Campbell heritage.

The *Declaration and Address* overflows with ideas of unity over division, peace rather than discord, inclusion instead of exclusion, and equality rather than inferiority. If these ideals were acknowledged and taken seriously by leaders in black Churches of Christ, what opportunity there would be for black men and black women to collaborate and work together, each bringing their gifts to bear in ministry. Instead of experiencing black women as problems to be dealt with, perhaps the idea of full communion would compel black church leaders to seek the cause of Christ rather than their own theological correctness. If theological correctness is understood as at the heart of the cause of Christ, our churches (both black and white) debate, judge, ostracize, and demean persons with alternate theological viewpoints, thus fostering division and engendering suspicion. However, in the *Declaration and Address,* Campbell urges Christians to make Christ the central figure in bringing about unity: "We would therefore, with all due deference and submission, call the attention of our brethren to the obvious and important duty of association....It is the cause of Christ and our brethren throughout all churches of catholic unity, peace, and purity—a cause that must finally prosper in spite of all opposition."[8]

The preceding statement crystallizes Thomas Campbell's belief that if unity was to occur among the churches, then Christians everywhere must possess the mind of Christ—leading each to esteem others better than themselves. For Christians in the twenty-first century, possessing this radical paradigm could give the church a fighting chance in eliminating many of the spiritual, social, and economic ills of our day, including sexism. After all, isn't this the image Christ created of the kingdom of God?

On more than one occasion, Christ's polemical message was one that upheld the cause of the poor, the oppressed, the prisoner, and the outsider. Certainly we remember his words of rebuke to the chief priests and elders in the Jerusalem temple, "Truly I tell you, the tax collectors and the prostitutes are going into the kingdom of God ahead of you" (Matt. 21:31, NRSV). While the religious leaders and political officials characterized tax collectors, sinners, and prostitutes as problems, Jesus enjoyed full communion with them. He talked with them, ate with them, and healed them. And they in turn gladly received his word. In fact, it was a foreigner in Luke 17:18 who praised God after being healed of his leprosy; it was a sinful woman in Luke 7 so overwhelmed with gratitude for being forgiven that she bathed the Lord's feet with her own tears and dried them with her hair; and it was an ostracized bleeding woman, desperate for a single touch from the Master, whom Jesus called daughter in Mark 5. Jesus' offer of full communion to the lost and the least reveals the heart of God and summons each of us to similarly enter into genuine fellowship with our neighbor. The Scriptures testify to the blessedness of the unity that results when we experience full communion. In Psalms the writer says, "How very good and pleasant it is when kindred live together in unity...for there the Lord ordained his blessing, life forevermore" (Psalm 133:1, NRSV).

Campbell's plea for full communion is, therefore, consistent with God's desire for unity, and is a sign of the inbreaking of the kingdom of God into the world. Christ's entrance into the world interrupted the status quo and set in motion an alternative vision for humanity. His presence and purpose on earth ushered in a new spiritual and ethical ethos characterized by faithful service and humble sacrifice on behalf of the world. For it was Jesus who declared that "whoever wishes to be great among you must be your servant, and whoever wishes to be first among you must be your slave; just as the Son of Man came not to be served but to serve, and to give his life a ransom for many" (Matt. 20:26, NRSV). It was Christ's recognition of his own purpose of service and sacrifice that enabled him to establish the agenda of the kingdom in Luke's gospel:

"The Spirit of the Lord is upon me, because he has anointed me to bring good news to the poor. He has sent me to proclaim release to the captives and recovery of sight to the blind, to let the oppressed go free, to proclaim the year of the Lord's favor" (Luke 4:18). Here Jesus outlines a ministry plan for those that would become his followers.

Can any of us deny that Paul, a follower of Christ, brought good news to the poor? Paul's message to the Gentiles was radically good news. No longer did Gentiles have to feel like second-class citizens because the kingdom of God through Christ was inclusive. Consequently, Gentiles could experience full communion with the Jews, and all those whom the Lord would call. Christ's vision was that the kingdom of God was to be one community of faith where distinctions of race, sex, and class posed no threat to one's ability to experience God's ideal of full communion with Christ and with one another.

The *Declaration and Address* is a prophetic document relevant even in the twenty-first century. It has an urgent message of inclusion that is antithetical to sexist and racist ideologies and characterizes the kingdom of God as a community where a young no-name black girl has the same privilege of full communion as a white church elder. Rather than seeing differences such as race, sex, and class as problems to be solved, the *Declaration and Address*, through its tenet of full communion, envisions a Christian community that considers theological difference as an opportunity to allow the cause of Christ to take center stage.

Toward that end, the cause of Christ is upheld when the good news is shared with the poor, the oppressed, and the blind, and when the captives are set free. Sexism as a form of oppression and injustice is antithetical to the cause of Christ. Sexism is a barrier to the experience of full communion and must be eliminated from all Christian Churches. It is divisive, demeaning, and destructive for all involved in its promulgation. By offering full communion to those considered by society as outsiders, Jesus went against the societal norms in promoting the full humanity of all people. Full communion is the acknowledgement of the full humanity in others. Therefore, full communion provides black women with the freedom to become all that God has created them to become and to do all that God has created them to do. In other words, full communion means black women no longer represent a problem to be dealt with. Instead, they become part of the solution.

For the Sake of the Gospel

Kei Eun Chang

Kei Eun Chang grew up in poverty in rural Korea where his mother, a Christian persecuted by her own family, prayed daily that he would become a minister. Though she died when he was only fifteen, Chang fulfilled his mother's desires, attending Seoul Christian University and later Emmanuel School of Religion. He has given his life to evangelism and church planting, now working to establish a Korean congregation in Manchester, New Hampshire. His struggles with the churches of the Stone-Campbell Movement have centered in two areas: the view held by most Korean Christians that our churches are strange, foreign, and insignificant; and the wrenching divisions among us that nullify the Movement's plea for the unity of all Christians and therefore block the spread of the gospel.

The challenge Kei Eun Chang issues in this call is to the churches and members of the Stone-Campbell Movement. Though dedicated to this movement within Christ's church, he sees through lenses that are very different from those worn by Americans and Westerners. His plea is on behalf of those who have not heard the gospel of Christ. Though parts of his "Declaration" may make us uncomfortable, we cannot avoid consideration of his urgings.

To the ministers, preachers, and evangelists of the Stone-Campbell heritage: Restore evangelistic sermons in your pulpit. Where there is no evangelistic fervor in the pulpit, the church becomes stagnant and declining. As the renowned theologian Emil Brunner said, "The church exists by mission as a fire exists by burning." When her members no longer hear soul-loving and soul-winning sermons, their spiritual power becomes like a dying fire. Further, as we remember and celebrate the Lord's Table each Sunday, we must also *remember* the mission of the church to those who are not around the Table; as we proclaim his death, we must remember the fact that Christ died for them as well. Therefore, on Sundays, we are reenergized in our love for the Lord and the evangelistic passion for his church.

To the Christian universities, colleges, and seminaries of our heritage: Instill in ministry and missionary students a passion for evangelism and practical training before they depart to their fields of harvest. Also support their further academic training in the best academic and theological institutions available to train promising scholarly leaders for the future of the churches of our heritage. Their scholarly voice will be important for the growth of our churches in the larger Christian context.

To the scholars, professors, and writers of the Restoration Movement: Continue to elevate the reputation of the churches of our heritage as you teach in renowned universities, colleges, and seminaries. I appreciate those scholars of the Stone-Campbell heritage such as Everett Ferguson, Leander Keck, Abraham Malherbe, Fred Craddock, M. Eugene Boring, Dale Martin, Carl Holliday, Michael White, and James

Walters, to name only a few in biblical studies. Their presence in the renowned mainline theological institutions as scholars who are members
of churches of the Stone-Campbell heritage
is significant particularly for Koreans among
whom the churches of our heritage are often
considered as "theologically unsound."

For instance, the scholarly contributions
of J. J. M. Roberts and Beverly Roberts Gaventa
of our tradition at Princeton Theological Seminary have made a tremendous difference for
good among Korean churches (Presbyterians
in particular) since Princeton is the most influential school among those bodies. Personally,
I wish I could see a note that Everett Ferguson

> "IT IS NOT THE
> VOICE OF THE
> MULTITUDE, BUT
> THE VOICE OF
> TRUTH, THAT HAS
> POWER WITH THE
> CONSCIENCE"

is of the Church of Christ on the cover page of the Korean version of
his influential *Backgrounds of Early Christianity*. This would be a drop
of water for Korean Christian Churches/Churches of Christ that are
overshadowed by the more powerful denominations, because almost all
Korean theological students know Ferguson's work. It is the same case
with Max Lucado, whose books are popular among Koreans. Though
almost all of his books have been published in Korean, most do not
indicate that the beloved pen of this best-selling writer and preacher
comes from a "strange tradition" called the "Church of Christ." When I
cite one of Lucado's works in my preaching, I intentionally mention that
he, who is loved by many Christians, is of our Restoration heritage.

To the leaders and scholars of the Restoration-Unity movement: We must understand ourselves theologically not simply as Churches of Christ/Christian Churches/Disciples of Christ that had a historical beginning in nineteenth-century America, but we also need to link our heritage to the church through the centuries all the way back to the first-century New Testament churches. If we have confidence that the churches of our heritage are truly churches that "Christ" established, we have to trace and develop a historical linkage back to Christ and to his faithful followers down to the nineteenth-century Restoration Movement, who raised their voices for establishing and handing down the church to us in spite of Satan's divisive activity in the history of the Christian Church. We have Christ as the commander of unity; Paul as the first "restorationist" who attempted to restore the purity and unity of the Corinthian church from its divisiveness; the many other reformers prior to the nineteenth century who attempted to preserve the unity and purity of Christ's church; and finally the voices of the nineteenth-century American church reformers at the climactic burst of our Restoration Movement.

Finally, we have to remove any obstacle for unity among us so that nothing will impede the way of the gospel beyond us. By "obstacle" among us, I do not mean what is biblically wrong or theologically unsound. Rather, I am talking about any potential barrier that may obstruct the mission of the churches of our heritage ("the way of the gospel") to the world. Our commitment to Christian unity, as conceived by Jesus, Paul, and Campbell, was for world evangelization. Thus, our concern for unity is not whether or not we need musical instruments in the worship, or whether or not we have to constitute a governing body and regulations for the churches of our heritage. Our concern is rather to make a *combined* effort to restore as many souls to God as possible.

However, it is true that the worship tradition of not using instruments among the churches of our heritage still provides a potential "obstacle" to the mission and the growth of the churches of our heritage. Some from this tradition use Paul's argument in 1 Corinthians that "it is permissible." However, Paul qualifies such Corinthian "knowledge" as not advantageous for the church, not because their *gnosis* or *exousia* (freedom) is wrong, but because it appears as an obstacle for the path of the gospel.

During our earlier years here in the Boston area, my family and I attended Brookline Church of Christ (a cappella) for a while. I enjoyed the congregation and even preached there, but even within my family, two sons who love music and play instruments felt uncomfortable with non-instrumental services. So my wife and I used to take them after the service to a Korean Presbyterian church service held in the afternoon just a few blocks away from Brookline Church of Christ. Another example involves a friend of mine whom I had met at school. He told me how much he and his Korean friends were attracted to the faithful Christian life of their American friends at a Church of Christ during his study in Nashville, Tennessee. Nevertheless, his family and others had to stop attending the worship services after just a few Sundays. He told me that it felt strange to have a service without instruments, and I cannot forget the question that he raised regarding his observation that all the members of the church were aged and that there were no young people in the church: "Doesn't this phenomenon stem from the fact that non-instrumental services serve to drive young men and women out of the church?" He thought so.

My practical suggestion on this matter is this: Instrumental Christian Churches/Churches of Christ, make plans to have services occasionally without instruments for the sake of our a cappella brothers and sisters so that we may together feel more closely the oneness among us. Though I have been mostly involved with the instrumental worship tradition, some of the most spiritual and truthful services that I have ever had were with non-instrumental churches.

Non-instrumental Churches of Christ, try to have services as often as you can with instruments for the same purpose, so that the breath of oneness prevails among us and, more importantly, that we together become a unified force for effective world evangelization. Forgive me if this hurts any brothers and sisters who still insist that a cappella singing is the only New Testament form of church worship service (I respect that opinion). By my suggestion here I do not mean to shake the biblical and hermeneutical foundation of non-instrumental services. To go back to Paul's directives, in his effort to solve another problem in the Corinthian worship service, he restricts speaking in

> "WE HAVE YOUR PRAYERS...LET US ALSO HAVE YOUR ASSISTANCE"

tongues in public services (1Cor. 14). Clearly, Paul does not reject speaking in tongues. Without mistake he considers it as a gift of the Spirit, and even recommends, "I would like all of you to speak in tongues, but" (14:5) he restricts it for the sake of "outsiders or nonbelievers" (14:23), namely, for evangelism. Back to my suggestion then: it is not a matter of whether this is biblical or not. Like Paul, I recommend continuing to keep the non-instrumental tradition with us; but do not dogmatize it for the sake of the gospel because non-instrumental services in our tradition appear as "obstacles" to our growth and to evangelism, particularly in the Korean context.

Therefore, let us consider Paul's *modus operandi* for evangelism: "I have made myself a slave to all, so that I might win more of them....To those *outside*...I became as one *outside*....To the weak I became weak, so that I might win the weak. I have become all things to all people, that I might by all means *save* some" (1Cor. 9:19-22, emphasis added). Paul makes it clear why he adopts the chameleon-like *modus operandi* for his mission: "I do it all *for the sake of the gospel*, so that I may share its blessings" to as many as possible (v. 23). He chooses not to exercise even what the law of Moses directs and what his Lord authorizes if it seems to be "an obstacle in the way of the gospel of Christ" (9:8-14). If then, can *we* (a cappella group) choose to use instruments in the service, even though it is not the form of the New Testament church service for us, *for the sake of the gospel*? Can *you* (instrumental brothers and sisters) choose not to use instruments in the service when a context demands to do so *for the sake of the gospel*? Am I stretching it too much if I suggest that we should adopt Paul's *modus operandi* for unity among ourselves and for our unified mission to the world?

In a recent interview in the wake of his retirement from the 40 years of ministry at Southeast Christian Church, a church that has a weekend attendance of 19,000, Bob Russell was asked, "How would you define 'unity' in the church?" His answer was: "We're not asking that they sing with instruments, nor are they asking that we sing without instruments. We want to recognize that we are brothers and we can work together to evangelize." Yes, we-can-work-together-to-evangelize the world should be the unifying force for the three branches of our biblically based heritage in the Stone-Campbell Movement.

Let me close with a famous Korean folk tale: A father had three sons. Knowing his sons easily became divisive even over trivial matters, he called for his three sons at his deathbed to speak his last important lesson. The father gave a stick to the eldest son and asked him to break it. He did the same with the other two sons. For each son, it was a piece of cake to break the stick. Now their father gave three sticks to each son and asked them to break those sticks; no son could do it. The father's lesson was simple, yet powerful: "Have no division among you! If you three are all of the same mind, nothing can defeat ("break") any of you, and in unity you can do whatever you want to do!" May I apply this story to the three streams ("three sons") of the Stone-Campbell Movement? Together ("in unity"), we can make a difference in America as well as in other parts of the world for Christ with his gospel. Together we can rebuild stagnant churches and plant new churches. Our "father"

(Thomas Campbell), I assume, would say to his three children if he could be invited as keynote speaker for our 2009 bicentennial celebration of his *Declaration and Address*, "This should be your unified vision for the twenty-first century and beyond."

PART 3
Communion Meditations

Communion Meditations

1.

When Jesus was with his disciples for a final meal, he said that one of them would betray him. He said it would be the one who dipped bread in his dish. The disciples began to question him, asking one after another, "Is it me?"

When we come and sit at the same table, there are essentials that we assume we have in common. Essentials like a belief in one Lord and one faith and one hope. These essentials form the basis of our fellowship. When I think of this kind of table, I cannot imagine that any division would exist there. I cannot imagine a betrayer being among us. Instead, my image of such a table is one where we all belong to each other, where we wish one another well, and where we genuinely value oneness.

I hope that the original disciples of Jesus had the same understanding. I believe that is why they became so upset when Jesus announced that one of them would betray him. Jesus was saying to that person that he was violating the meaning of the Table. The betrayer did not understand the essentials of oneness and so did not really understand the Table.

As we come together at the Lord's Table, it is an expression of the unity that exists among us. Participation at the Table makes the unity come to life. And the oneness we share becomes real.

MORDICAI CHIKWANDA, ZIMBABWE

2.

Since I have had the opportunity to minister in over twenty countries, I know something of the variety of worship practices around the world. While there are many styles of worship in Stone-Campbell churches, the one practice common to all is the celebration of communion. The Table is where we find our unity.

One of the most moving incidents I have experienced during communion was in Papua New Guinea. It was hot and humid that Sunday morning and we were sitting on small logs. As prayers of thanksgiving were being offered, I began to drift off. But I was awakened by the sound of soft crying. The woman leading us in prayer was so deeply concerned about her sins that she was pouring out her heart to God and seeking the forgiveness we find in Christ. The emotion of her prayer brought me to tears as well and caused me to consider my own motivations at the Table.

Sometimes the Table is a place for tears, other times a place for joy. Mother Teresa once said that she found the strength to love all people because, for her, each one looked like Jesus. Whether in our joy or in our sorrow, we come to communion knowing that we are accepted because of our resemblance to Christ.

We are truly brothers and sisters—one family. We are all God's children. In Christ we are cleansed through laughter and tears, so that we can share the same unity enjoyed by the Father and his Son. Let us celebrate our place in God's kingdom. Let us celebrate as family in happy times and sad times. Let us come to the Table.

JEFF WESTON, AUSTRALIA

Courtesy of Ted Parks

More than Meets the Eye

At first glance this photograph depicts what is seen each week at countless congregations of the Stone-Campbell Movement around the world –the Lord's Supper. However, closer examination shows that this brief moment in time captures the reality of the diversity and uniqueness of our changing global community.

Here Dr. Peter Shenoudah, left, a visually-impaired Christian, is assisted in partaking of the Lord's Supper by Nadiha Francis, both natives of Egypt and members of Lakeshore Christian Church, a congregation of the Christian Churches. They are being served by Thomas Kleinert, a native of Germany and senior minister of Vine Street Christian Church (Disciples of Christ) and Sara Harwell, member of the Natchez Trace Church of Christ, a congregation of the Churches of Christ.

This observance of the Lord's Supper took place as part of the Stone-Campbell Dialogue Worship Service on June 11, 2006—the year in which the 100th anniversary of the split between Churches of Christ and Disciples of Christ was observed and during which significant steps towards reconciliation were initiated. The event, which was hosted by congregations of all three streams of the Movement in Nashville, Tennessee, took place at the Woodmont Hills Church of Christ. Thomas Campbell calls us to remember that the Lord's Supper is "that great ordinance of unity and love!" (Photo courtesy of Ted Parks)

3.

As Disciples we spread the Table of the Lord every Sunday. We consider the partaking of the bread and cup as the most important portion of the worship service.

The idea of "table" was more meaningful in the age of the Apostles than it is today. To eat together indicated an acceptance of each other as brothers and sisters. Since all of life was related to the worship of God, to invite a person to your table was to recognize that everyone is related to God. And then to receive the invitation from the Lord himself meant that he saw us as part of his family and held us in his heart.

At the Lord's Table we experience a spiritual oneness with God and with our fellow believers. Indeed, it is the fellowship of the Table that heals all wounds and brings a forgiving spirit into our hearts. The Apostle Paul said to the church in Corinth that each of us should examine himself before coming to the Table, so that any unforgiveness harboring itself in our hearts could be dispelled before joining with others at the Lord's Table. As we release everything hindering us from full communion, then we can find the spiritual oneness that is offered at the Table.

Let us always remember that when we come together at the Lord's Table, we come by invitation. And we know that Christ is giving the same invitation to people everywhere. At the Table we accept each other as brothers and sisters—we see that we are all a part of God's family. And we enjoy the presence of Christ in our hearts.

PETRUS MARYONO, INDONESIA

4.

As the first day comes every week, we come to the Table at Christ's invitation. The Lord's Supper is one of the acts of true worship. In remembering Christ at the Table, we experience the bond of Christian fellowship because, although we are many different people, we participate at the Table with one mind and one faith.

It was during a festival that our Lord instituted communion. He asked us to remember him each time we come together at the Table. And so we recall Christ's death and resurrection; we once again feel his love and hear his name; we remember his affliction, but we also see his exaltation. We know that we will live forever because of the resurrection of Christ.

Just as first-century Christians followed the pattern that had been given them, we too hold to the purposes given to us by the Apostle Paul and the other New Testament writers. Just as they came to communion with the same mind and faith, we come in the unity that we find in Christ.

We know that some Christians celebrate communion only infrequently. But we believe that the Lord is calling us to the Table each and every Sunday. The Lord's Supper was given so that we could know our sins have been forgiven. Just as we obey the Lord in the rest of our life, we obey him as well by coming to his Table each week.

At the Table we live out a true act of worship. The symbols of our Lord's body are there. They remind us of who Christ is. And they remind us of who we are.

VINAY KUMAR, INDIA

5.

One day when I was serving in the island nation of Vanuatu in the South Pacific, the members of the Christian Women's Fellowship decided to have a parade. The women from Pentekost Island wore a gorgeous green, while those from Port Vila were in pink. Others paraded in purple or bright yellow.

Me? I had on a dark blue dress. When we all gathered for a group photo, Evelyn, the CWF president, took me quickly inside a nearby house. "We want you to stand out in a bright color, too," she said. I pulled off my dark blue dress and slipped on the bright yellow one offered to me.

We dashed back to find our place in the parade. I found myself in bright yellow amidst a sea of beautiful colors. How wonderful to be included in the colorful parade and for all the women to accept me as part of God's family.

Christ calls for all of us to join the parade. No matter which colors we are wearing, we shine with the light of his Spirit as we walk along hand-in-hand.

The same is true as we come to the communion table. No one is excluded. We are all welcome. We are all part of God's family. Let's put on our best yellow and green and purple and pink, and parade to the Lord's Table together. Christ has invited us and waits for us with our sea of colors.

ANA GOBLEDALE, UNITED STATES

Notes

Essentially, Intentionally and Constitutionally One

[1] There are three book-length biographies of Thomas Campbell: Alexander Campbell's *Memoirs of Thomas Campbell* (Cincinnati, OH: H.S. Bosworth, 1861 and 1871), William Herbert Hanna, *Thomas Campbell, Seceder and Christian Union Advocate* (Cincinnati, OH: Standard Publishing, 1935; reprint ed., College Press, 1986); and Lester McAllister, *Thomas Campbell, Man of the Book* (St. Louis, MO: Bethany Press, 1954).

[2] Traveling with Thomas Campbell was Miss Hannah Acheson whom Thomas was escorting to her family in Pennsylvania. Hannah was the first love of Alexander Campbell and is an interesting footnote to Disciple history.

[3] A Postscript was added before final publication.

[4] Alexander dated the event to October 1809 in "Anecdotes, Incidents and Facts," *Millennial Harbinger* (May 1848), 280. "The first *proof sheet* that I ever read was a form of my father's Declaration and Address, in press in Washington, Pennsylvania, on my arrival there in October, 1809." The incident is cited in reference to his conclusion of the unscriptural nature of infant baptism.

[5] See Eva Jean Wrather, *Alexander Campbell, Adventurer in Freedom* (Fort Worth, TX: Texas Christian University Press, 2005), for an in-depth account of Alexander Campbell's life.

[6] Alexander Campbell later commented that it, "indeed, had a very limited circulation." *Millennial Harbinger,* "Good News From a Far Country" (June 1846), 230.

[7] H. Eugene Johnson, *The Declaration and Address for Today* (Nashville, TN: Reed and Company, 1971), 11. Others have made similar assertions. Thomas Acheson, whose signature appears on page 23 of the original edition, was the uncle of Hannah Acheson. The Acheson family had long been friends of the Campbells in Ireland.

[8] Lester McAllister, *Thomas Campbell, Man of the Book* (St. Louis, MO: Bethany Press), 138.

[9] Thomas Campbell, "Christian Union," *Millennial Harbinger (*March 1839), 142-143. On one or two other occasions in the *Millennial Harbinger* Thomas Campbell mentions oppositions and "verbal contentions" to his reform agenda.

[10] Robert Richardson, *Memoirs of Alexander Campbell* (Philadelphia: J.B. Lippincott & Company, 1868), see chapter XIV, pages 247-275; quote taken from page 273.

[11] McAllister, *Thomas Campbell*, 141-142.

[12] Accurate statistics in the early period of the Movement are difficult to ascertain. It was not until 1880 that the American Christian Missionary Society could report to the Federal Census any sort of systematic enumeration. Totals for 1880 show 5,100 churches and 591,821 members in 39 states and territories (U.S.). Grant K. Lewis, *The American Christian Missionary Society* (St. Louis, MO: Christian Board of Publication, 1937), 144, 205.

[13] Alexander Campbell, *The Christian System*, 3rd edition (Pittsburg, PA: Forrester and Campbell, 1840), 8.

[14] Alexander Campbell, *Memoirs of Elder Thomas Campbell*, H.S. Bosworth, Cincinnati, Ohio, 1861), iv.

[15] Lester G. McAllister, "Thomas Campbell," *The Encyclopedia of the Stone-Campbell Movement*, (Grand Rapids, MI: William B. Eerdmans, 2004).

[16] Thomas Campbell does not indicate who attended the "Convention" other than a "respectable number of ministers and others." *Millennial Harbinger*, "Christian Union" (March 1839), 134-144.

[17] A "second" bound 1809 copy is also housed at Bethany College but, according to Archivist Jeanne Cobb, is not considered to be a copy published for distribution in 1809. Email to the author, January 16, 2007. A second "proof sheet" copy or "page proof" was allegedly known to have existed in the Library of Overdale College, Birmingham, England in the 1930s. See footnote, Dean E. Walker's *Adventuring for Christian Unity*, printed in England, 1935, page 20; subsequently reprinted in *Adventuring for Christian Unity and Other Essays* (Johnson City, TN: Emmanuel School of Religion, 1992). Other references have been noted referring to this "page proof." The Archives of the British Churches of Christ are housed in the Central Library of the Selly Oak Colleges in Birmingham, England. Presently, existence of this "page proof" has not been verified.

[18] For a discussion of the Alexander Campbell corrections—largely spelling, punctuation, capitalization, word division, and typography—see http://www.mun. ca.rels.restmov/texts/campbell/da/DA-1ST.htm

[19] Richardson, *Memoirs of Alexander Campbell*. Eva Jean Wrather's *Alexander Campbell, Adventurer in Freedom, A Literary Biography*, was completed in 1945 but is only now appearing in print. Volumes I and II have been released as a joint project

of TCU Press, Fort Worth, and Disciples of Christ Historical Society. Unfortunately, neither cites sources.

[20] Charles Alexander Young, *Historical Documents Advocating Christian Union,*(Chicago, IL: Christian Century Company, 1904), 8-9, 36.

[21] See W. R. Warren's personal papers located at Disciples of Christ Historical Society, Nashville, Tennessee, as well as extensive files on the Centennial Convention itself.

[22] Produced by the Centennial Committee, Pittsburgh, in 1908; Numbers 1, 2 and 16 of the zinc etching reprint are housed in the Archives and Special Collections, T.W. Phillips Memorial Library, Bethany College, Bethany, West Virginia. Copy number 53 is in the collection of the author. It is unknown if the Record Publishing Company of Coraopolis is related to the "Record" of the 1809 edition.

[23] Letter found inside copy of the book in the library of the Disciples of Christ Historical Society, Nashville, Tennessee.

[24] Dean E. Walker, *Adventuring for Christian Unity* (Cincinnati, OH: Standard Publishing, 1935), 20; Reproduced in Dean Walker, *Adventuring for Christian Unity*, 379.

[25] *Centennial Convention Report* (Cincinnati, OH: Standard Publishing Company, undated). Publisher's Note is located at the first of the book, the five essays begin on page 349; Willett's begins on page 356.

[26] Frederick Doyle Kershner, *The Christian Union Overture: An Interpretation of the Declaration and Address of Thomas Campbell* (St. Louis, MO: Bethany Press, 1923).

[27] Quoted in Johnson, *The Declaration and Address for Today*, 9. Quoted from an uncited *Christian Standard* article.

[28] Pearl Howard Welshimer, *Concerning the Disciples* (Cincinnati, OH: Standard Publishing, 1935), 53-55. *Concerning the Disciples* enjoyed multiple reprints for several years and was the standard history book of the Movement for the layman in the mid-twentieth century, perhaps due in part to Welshimer's own popularity.

[29] William Robinson, *Declaration and Address by Thomas Campbell*, With An Introduction by William Robinson (Birmingham, England: Berean Press, 1951), iii-iv, 22. Robinson also noted that a first edition of the *Declaration and Address* was housed in the Library of Overdale College, Birmingham, England, where he was principal, 1920-1949.

[30] Johnson, *The Declaration and Address for Today*, 4.

[31] H. Eugene Johnson, *The Current Reformation: Thoughts from Thomas Campbell* (privately printed, 1972), 3 (Foreword by Charles R. Gresham).

[32] The Gospel Advocate Company of Nashville, Tennessee, also reprinted and made available many long-out-of-date books and periodicals of the early Restoration Movement.

[33] Knofel Staton, *The Paraphrase of Thomas Campbell's Declaration and Address* (Joplin, MO: College Press, 1976). The paraphrase is available online thanks to Dr. Knofel Staton and Ernie Stefanik at:

http://www.mun.ca./rels/restmov/texts/tcampbell/etc/DA-KS.HTM

[34] The Restoration Movement website overseen by Hans Rollmann can be found listed above.

[35] Thomas H. Olbricht and Hans Rollmann, *The Quest for Christian Unity, Peace, and Purity in Thomas Campbell's Declaration and Address: Text and Studies* (Lanham, MD, and London: Scarecrow Press, 2000).

[36] Douglas A. Foster, Anthony L. Dunnavant, Paul M. Blowers, D. Newell Williams, Editors, *The Encyclopedia of the Stone-Campbell Movement* (Grand Rapids, MI: William B. Eerdmans, 2004).

The Problem of Full Communion

[1] W. E. B. Dubois, *The Souls of Black Folk* (New York: Penguin Books, 1989), 3-4.

[2] I represent myself as black rather than African-American in order to connect myself to all women of African decent.

[3] "The Negro in Worship," available from http://www.mun.ca/rels/restmov/texts/race/negro.html.

[4] Ibid.

[5] Ibid.

[6] Ibid.

[7] "Declaration and Address by Thomas Campbell"; available from http://www.mun.ca/rels/restmov/texts/tcampbell/da/DA-1st.HTM.

[8] Campbell, "The Declaration and Address," section 14.

Contributors

GLENN THOMAS CARSON is President of Disciples of Christ Historical Society, Nashville, Tennessee.

VICTOR KNOWLES is President of Peace on Earth Ministries, Joplin, Missouri, and Editor of *One Body* magazine.

CLINTON J. HOLLOWAY is a historian and shares in the ministry of World Convention, Nashville, Tennessee.

DOUGLAS A. FOSTER is Associate Dean of the Graduate School of Theology, Abilene Christian University, Abilene, Texas.

RICK GROVER is Lead Pastor of Journey Christian Church, Metairie, Louisiana.

AMY LIGNITZ HARKEN is Senior Minister of First Christian Church (Disciples of Christ), Independence, Missouri.

DANIEL A. RODRIQUEZ is Associate Professor of Religion and Hispanic Studies, Pepperdine University, Malibu, California.

GREG TAYLOR is Associate Minister of Garnett Church of Christ, Tulsa, Oklahoma, and editor of *New Wineskins* magazine.

IRIE LYNNE SESSION is Associate Area Minister, North Texas Area of the Christian Church (Disciples of Christ) in the Southwest, Fort Worth, Texas.

KEI EUN CHANG ministers with Manchester Korean Christian Church, Manchester, New Hampshire.

JEFF WESTON, Australia

VINAY KUMAR, India

PETRUS MARYONO, Indonesia

MORDICAI CHIKWANDA, Zimbabwe

ANA GOBLEDALE, United States